Numbers

Paul W. Kuske

CPH.
SAINT LOUIS

The interior illustrations were originally executed by James Tissot (1836–1902). The diagram on page 27 was done by Northwestern Publishing House artist Kurt Adams and the map on page 249 by John Lawrenz.

Commentary and pictures are reprinted from NUMBERS (The People's Bible Series), copyright © 1990 by Northwestern Publishing House. Used by permission.

Scripture taken from the HOLY BIBLE, NEW INTERNATIONAL VERSION ®. NIV ®. Copyright © 1973, 1978, 1984 by the International Bible Society. Used by permission of Zondervan Publishing House. All rights reserved.

Copyright © 1996 Concordia Publishing House
3558 S. Jefferson Avenue, St. Louis, MO 63118-3968
Manufactured in the United States of America

1 2 3 4 5 6 7 8 9 10   05 04 03 02 01 00 99 98 97 96

CONTENTS

ILLUSTRATIONS

PREFACE

The People's Bible Commentary is just what the name implies—a Bible and commentary for the people. It includes the complete text of the Holy Scriptures in the popular New International Version. The commentary following the Scripture sections contains personal applications as well as historical background and explanations of the text.

The authors of *The People's Bible Commentary* are men of scholarship and practical insight, gained from years of experience in the teaching and preaching ministries. They have tried to avoid the technical jargon which limits so many commentary series to professional Bible scholars.

The most important feature of these books is that they are Christ-centered. Speaking of the Old Testament Scriptures, Jesus himself declared, "These are the Scriptures that testify about me" (John 5:39). Each volume of *The People's Bible Commentary* directs our attention to Jesus Christ. He is the center of the entire Bible. He is our only Savior.

We dedicate these volumes to the glory of God and to the good of his people.

The Publishers

Moses

NUMBERS
INTRODUCTION

Thirty-five centuries ago two million people wandered in the Sinai desert and miraculously received manna from God each day. Others had wandered there and died of starvation. Two million people prospered because they were the people chosen by God. At that same time other millions also prospered in the ancient Near East and made their marks on the pages of history, but the Bible makes little mention of them. During that same period of time empires were rising and falling in other parts of the world. The Lord's attention, however, was focused on that relative handful of people he was leading from Egypt to Canaan. To them he gave victory after victory.

The biblical account focuses on this one nation because they were the descendants of Abraham. They were the people with whom God had made a solemn contract, a covenant. In it he gave his word that the Savior promised to Abraham would come from this people. That promise was reason enough for the detailed biblical record of God's loving care for this people.

The book of Numbers presents a crucial thirty-nine year segment of the history of this covenant people. The historical record in Numbers spans the years from the time the Israelites encamped at Mt. Sinai to their encampment on the plains east of the Jordan River a generation later.

Theme

"The Lord is with us!" (Numbers 14:9) That was the confident plea of Joshua and Caleb, two of the twelve spies

1

who had been sent to explore Canaan. "If the Lord is pleased with us, he will lead us into that land," expresses the faith of the two spies. They hung on to this hope in spite of the fact that the majority of the Israelites followed the negative report of the other ten spies and refused to go forward in the name of the Lord.

"The LORD is with us!" This statement expressed the confidence that the Lord had demonstrated his presence to the Children of Israel in many ways. He had given them victory after victory and promised even more victories. He had led them through a series of difficulties to the borders of the land flowing with milk and honey. Each day he had miraculously provided food and water in a strange and frightening wilderness. Day by day he continued to show his presence by means of a pillar of cloud by day and a pillar of fire by night. He instructed the people in their worship life. He was providing the standards by which their nation was to function. On many occasions he showed he was as concerned about individuals as he was about the whole nation. The evidence overwhelmingly supported Caleb's confident statement: "The LORD is with us!"

Yet the reaction of the Israelites stands in stark contrast to the confident trust of Joshua and Caleb. How fickle they were! How frail their trust in the Lord! While there were moments when they did serve the Lord faithfully, there was also a long series of complaints and rebellions against him. Moses tells us the rebelliousness reached its climax at a place called Kadesh, near the southern border of Canaan. The people refused to follow the confident urging of Caleb and Joshua. They refused to enter the promised land because they accepted the negative report of the ten spies. By refusing to believe God's promise they forfeited the privilege of taking possession of the land. That decision (chapter 14) is the turning point of the book.

Prior to that point the book of Numbers records a growing tension between the Lord and the people. The Lord was faithful, but among the people we see dissatisfaction and rebelliousness growing and festering.

Even after the turning point the faithfulness of the Lord was still very evident in all that follows. That is why he continued to discipline the people. Consequently, after wandering in the wilderness for thirty-eight years after their rebellion, the people of Israel were far less rebellious. Although they continued to disobey the Lord at times, the people seemed more willing to follow the Lord and claim the new homeland he had promised them. In confidence they arrived at the Jordan River. Their mood at the river bank reflected the attitude of Joshua and Caleb. They now accepted the truth: "The LORD is with us!"

Outline

The four natural divisions of the book of Numbers are based on the geographical areas in which the children of Israel were encamped. They are: (1) from Sinai to Kadesh; (2) the years of wandering; (3) from Kadesh to the Jordan River; (4) preparations at the Jordan River.

In connection with each of these geographical areas Moses dwells on three or four related topics (1) life in the community; (2) life as individuals; (3) life in worship; and (4) life while moving out. In the first and last part of the book Moses chose to write about all four topics. In the two middle sections, he chose to include only three of the topics. These observations suggest the following outline:

Theme: "The LORD is with us!"

I. From Sinai to Kadesh (chapters 1-14)
  A. Life in the community (1-4)
     Census of the entire nation; camp arrangement; census and responsibilities of the Levites

B. Life while moving out (31)
Vengeance on the Midianites; spoils
C. Life in the community (32:1-35:5)
The transjordan tribes; review of stages of the desert journey; boundaries of Canaan; towns of the Levites
D. Life as individuals (35:6-36:13)
Cities of refuge; second request of Zelophehad's daughters

Title

When we call the fourth book of the Old Testament "Numbers," we are following the Septuagint. (The Septuagint is a translation of the Old Testament Hebrew into Greek and was made about 285 B.C.) The Septuagint translators wished to indicate that the book records several numberings of the children of Israel.

These numberings were especially important on two occasions. The first counting occurred at Mount Sinai and included all the men who were twenty years old or older when the Israelites came out of Egypt and who were fit to go to war. The second important counting occurred a generation later at the Jordan River. At that point it was determined that the entire generation of men (except for Joshua and Caleb) who had been counted at the first census had died. The Lord's judgment on an unfaithful generation had been carried out.

Unfortunately the title, "Numbers," has led many people to believe that the whole book is made up of dull statistics. Perhaps people would more readily read this book if we followed the custom of the children of Israel. They used the first word of each book as its title. The title of Numbers then would be "In the Wilderness." How neatly that summarizes the content of the book! It traces the history of the people of God during those thirty-nine years they wandered from Mount Sinai to the Jordan River. More precisely, the book of Numbers shows how God protected, blessed, disciplined, provided for, forgave and led the children of Israel while they were in the wilderness. The book ends on the happy note that the Lord, the God of free and faithful grace, had after four centuries kept his promise to Abraham. The Israelites were encamped at the Jordan River, ready to claim the land promised centuries earlier to Abraham for his descendants.

Historical Setting

All dates in Numbers are defined in terms of the escape from Egypt or the departure from Mount Sinai. There is no specific reference to external events that might help us determine the exact time of the events described. On the other hand, since the dates are determined by the events recorded in Exodus, we will set the date of the Israelites' departure from Egypt at about 1446 B.C. and the departure from Mount Sinai as one year later. For more details on the matter of the dating the reader may wish to check pages 5 and 6 of the Exodus volume of *The People's Bible*.

Author

The statement "God spoke to Moses" occurs at least eighty times in the book of Numbers. Another hundred times we are merely told that God spoke. It is therefore obvious to conclude that Moses wrote down what God told him. In fact, in Numbers 33:2 the Lord specifically commanded Moses to write down a list of the "stages" of the journey in the desert. At other times God's instructions were so detailed that it is only natural to assume that Moses, who had the privilege of talking to God face to face, simply wrote them down.

At the time of Christ this book had been included in the collection of five books that were entitled "The Law of Moses." (To be more precise the Hebrew term really means "The Instructions of Moses.") Consequently, every reference in the New Testament to the "Law of Moses" is additional evidence that God does indeed consider Moses the author of the fourth book of the Bible. Christ himself put his stamp of approval on the accuracy of Numbers when he said to Nicodemus, "Just as Moses lifted up the snake in the desert, so the Son of Man must be lifted up" (John 3:14; see Numbers 21:4-9).

Moses the Mediator of the Old Covenant

The Lord himself chose Moses to be the greatest of the prophets. Of him the Lord said:

"When a prophet of the LORD is among you,
    I reveal myself to him in visions,
    I speak to him in dreams.
But this is not true of my servant Moses;
    he is faithful in all my house.
With him I speak face to face,
    clearly and not in riddles;
    he sees the form of the LORD" (Numbers 12:6-8).

What a remarkably clear expression of the special position God assigned to Moses! The Lord himself expands on the superiority of Moses by showing the direct relationship between Moses and Christ in the familiar prophecy: "The LORD your God will raise up for you a prophet like me from among your own brothers. You must listen to him" (Deuteronomy 18:15; see also v. 18). The parallel between Moses and the prophet to come is noteworthy. Yet the words also

7

point to the superiority of that coming prophet (Jesus) as the one who deserves our full attention.

Another parallel between the work of Moses and of Christ is that both served as *mediators* between sinners and the holy God. In the New Testament the term *mediator* is used a number of times to draw the parallels and contrasts between Moses and Christ. Both functioned as God's mediator to bring messages to man. Both also functioned as mediator for man, taking man's needs and requests before the Lord of heaven. We identify these two functions with the prophetic and the priestly offices.

It is in the prophetic function that Moses again and again announced to the people the will of God. The instructions he had to give at the command of the Lord ranged from the building of the Tent of Meeting to the census and to the judgment on a man who gathered sticks on the Sabbath. Whenever the Israelites carried out the will of the Lord, Moses carefully noted their obedience. The phrase-by-phrase repetition of the instructions showed the meticulous care with which the children of Israel were to obey the Lord. It may seem tedious to us but there can be no question about their obedience. All of this underscores the faithfulness with which Moses carried out his commission as a prophet of the Lord.

Moses also functioned as priest. Before the priesthood of Aaron was established, Moses did the sacrificing. We are told that he functioned as priest at the dedication of the Tent of Meeting (Exodus 40:29). Moses performed another priestly function when he acted as an intercessor on behalf of the people. Whether he was pleading for the people who had worshipped the golden calf (Exodus 32:1ff), or presenting the need for water before the Lord (Numbers 20:6), or pleading for the Israelites when they had refused to go forward into the Promised Land (Numbers 14:13ff), Moses often acted as the spokesman of the people before the Lord. Indeed, on one occasion he expressed his willingness to forfeit his own salvation, if by so doing he could save his people (Exodus 32:32).

There is also a parallel with the kingly office of Christ. Moses was the political leader of the people of Israel. Under God's direction he gave them their marching orders (Numbers 9:23). He was their judge, though he needed the help of others (Exodus 18:15ff). On another occasion he was directed to appoint seventy elders to help him in his administrative duties (Numbers 11:16-25). In the kingly office Moses functioned as the servant of the Lord to keep order among the people of Israel.

So Moses combined the offices of prophet, priest and king in his own person. As time went on the priestly function was handed over to Aaron and his descendants. At the time of Moses' death the kingly function was handed over to Joshua. Whenever God sent prophets in the years that followed, the prophetic office was then continued.

Yet as remarkable as the parallel between the work of Moses and of Christ is, the superiority of Christ is also very clear. Christ is an eternal prophet, priest and king. When he spoke he did so not as a mouthpiece of someone else; he spoke on his own prophetic authority as the Son of God. He made a single, sinless sacrifice that suffices for all ages, functioning both as the victim and as the priest. He also rules through all ages as the King of kings and Lord of lords, so that the gates of hell will not prevail against his church.

But the superiority of Christ does not diminish the high honor the Lord placed on Moses. The covenant he mediated had its own level of glory. That level of glory is demonstrated in the fact that the face of Moses shone whenever he came from the presence of the Lord at the Tent of Meeting (2 Corinthians 3:7ff). The fact that the face of Moses had a temporary glow served God's grace-filled purposes in the period prior to the coming of Christ.

While it is true that the Old Testament covenant was filled with shadows and pictures of the coming Christ, it did carry the message of forgiveness for fallen man. Therefore though we as people of the New Testament can rejoice in the full reality of Christ's redemptive work, the daily sacrifices and the sacrifices on the great Day of Atonement brought the same redemptive message to the people who lived before Christ. Though we know that the one sacrifice of Christ is sufficient for all time, the mere fact of repetition was a constant instruction to Old Testament believers reminding them that without the shedding of blood as a redemption there is no forgiveness of sins (Hebrews 9:22). Those Old Testament blood sacrifices were all shadows that pointed to the sacrifice that Christ would make.

Truly Moses enjoyed a high privilege as he communicated God's message to the people of God. That revelation was the foundation of God's covenant for 1500 years. Only the revelation of Christ supplanted it (Hebrews 1:1-4). The priesthood and the sacrifices, which were instituted at the time of Moses, were a focal point in God's dealings with the Old Testament believers. Only the priesthood and the sacrifice of Christ himself could supersede what God had established through Moses (Hebrews 7:20ff; 9:23). In the forty years of Moses' ministry the Lord established the Old Covenant. Only in another forty year period that included our Savior's life would a "superior" covenant be established (Hebrews 8:6).

Indeed even in the events of Moses' life there are interesting parallels to the life of Christ. For example, both were rescued from the murderous designs of an evil king (Exodus 2:2-10; Matthew 2:14,15). Other parallels are: miracles involving water (Exodus 14:21; Matthew 8:26); feeding a multitude (Exodus 16:15; Matthew 14:20-21). Both had radiant faces (Exodus 34:35; Matthew 17:2), were discredited among their countrymen (Numbers 12:1ff; John 7:5), and made intercessory prayers for the people (Exodus 32:32; John 17:9). Both had seventy helpers (Numbers 11:16-17; Luke 10:1), and reappeared after death (Matthew 17:3; Acts 1:3).

Truly in many ways Moses was a special instrument of the Lord. In Numbers we will be able to observe him as he worked in the Lord's service.

Impact

The events that are recorded in Numbers burned themselves deeply into the minds of the children of Israel. Again and again the prophets and psalmists reminded the people not to test the Lord in the way that the Israelites had done in the wilderness. Echoes of that admonition run through both the Old and New Testaments. Even today the rebellion of the children of Israel at Kadesh stands as a solemn warning to us.

On the other hand, the book of Numbers also shows the faithfulness and power of God. To those who serve him he will gladly pour out rich blessings. Through all ages believers can exclaim with Joshua and Caleb, "The LORD is with us!"

Purpose

The obvious purpose of Numbers is to record the historical events that occurred while the children of Israel traveled from Sinai to the Jordan River. In fulfilling that purpose the book narrates incidents that happened at various campsites. But the fact that no events are recorded at some campsites also shows that this is a selective account of the spiritual history of the children of Israel.

Because it is a spiritual history we should not be surprised that Moses takes us from the joyous emotional heights the people experienced at the dedication of the tabernacle and at the first celebration of the Passover, down through their growing criticism of God to the depths of their refusal to go forward into Canaan at the Lord's direction. Then we understand the thirty-eight years of chastisement that passed between the first and second encampment at Kadesh. Following the enforced stay in the wilderness God's continued blessing stands in sharp contrast to the events showing unfaithfulness of the people. Again and again throughout the book the theme is clearly there: "The LORD is with us."

So rising above the actions and reactions of Israel we see the history of God's love in dealing with his chosen people. Throughout this whole period God remained completely faithful. Although the people tested his patience many times, God still called them his chosen nation. In spite of their repeated acts of rebellion God preserved the nation in order to carry out his gracious plan to provide the Savior. Under the grand and over-arching purpose of sending the Messiah, the Lord provided food for his people in a miraculous way; he gave them many victories; he protected the soldiers in battle; he frustrated a conniving false prophet and finally brought the children of Israel to the land of promise.

As we study the book of Numbers we will focus on the Lord and on his faithfulness. That is what Joshua and Caleb wanted to proclaim to the people when they said, "The LORD is with us!" (Numbers 14:9) They were ready to go forward with such confidence in the Lord. May this rallying cry strengthen us as it has strengthened the faithful in all ages!

PART I
FROM SINAI TO KADESH

NUMBERS 1—14

The first part of Numbers moves from the events at Mount Sinai to the rebellion at Kadesh. While the children of Israel were at Mount Sinai, the Lord did require them to count the men who were twenty years old or more and were fit for war. The Lord's rich blessing on the descendants of Abraham was obvious.

On the basis of the census, the Lord also designated the position of the various tribes in the camp. The camp was designed to focus inward on the Tent of Meeting, which was surrounded by the Levites. In the outer circle were the people of the various tribes. The Lord also gave the instructions for a counting of the Levites and gave specific responsibilities to each of the Levite clans.

Life in the Community

The first four chapters of Numbers focus on matters that were important to the whole community. The numbering of the people showed how well God had kept his promise to make a great nation from the descendants of Abraham. That such a large company of people might proceed in an orderly way, it was also vital that an orderly arrangement for the camp should be made. For the worship life of the community there is also a definition of the responsibilities of the priests and the Levites.

A Census Commanded

1 The LORD spoke to Moses in the Tent of Meeting in the Desert of Sinai on the first day of the second month of the second year after the Israelites came out of Egypt. He said: ²"Take a census of the whole Israelite community by their clans and families, listing every man by name, one by one. ³You and Aaron are to number by their divisions all the men in Israel twenty years old or more who are able to serve in the army. ⁴One man from each tribe, each the head of his family, is to help you. ⁵These are the names of the men who are to assist you:

> from Reuben, Elizur son of Shedeur;
> ⁶from Simeon, Shelumiel son of Zurishaddai;
> ⁷from Judah, Nahshon son of Amminadab;
> ⁸from Issachar, Nethanel son of Zuar;
> ⁹from Zebulon, Eliab son of Helon;
> ¹⁰from the sons of Joseph:
> > from Ephraim, Elishama son of Ammihud;
> > from Manasseh, Gamaliel son of Pedahzur;
> ¹¹from Benjamin, Abidan son of Gideoni;
> ¹²from Dan, Ahiezer son of Ammishaddai;
> ¹³from Asher, Pagiel son of Ocran;
> ¹⁴from Gad, Eliasaph son of Deuel;
> ¹⁵from Naphtali, Ahira son of Enan."

¹⁶These were the men appointed from the community, the leaders of their ancestral tribes. They were the heads of the clans of Israel.

The tone for the entire book of Numbers is set in the very first words: "The LORD spoke to Moses." That phrase is repeated at least eighty times in the book. Very clearly the life of the people, the two censuses, the instructions for the worship life and the decisions for moving from campsite to campsite were under the direct supervision of the Lord.

The book of Numbers reports again and again that the Lord used Moses as his spokesman. In face to face communication the Lord spoke to Moses at the Tent of Meeting. Over that tent the Lord hovered in a cloud by day and in a pillar of fire by night. So when the Lord wanted to speak to Moses, he summoned him to the tent and addressed him there.

The place and time when the Lord spoke to Moses is clearly noted in the opening statement of the book. The time was the first day of the second month of the second year after the people had been delivered from Egypt. The children of Israel were still encamped at the foot of Mount Sinai. Comparing this dating with Exodus and Leviticus it is clear that the events in the first part of Numbers are closely related to the dedication of the Tent of Meeting. The dedicatory celebration had begun on the first day of the second year (See Exodus 40.) Further, the events in the book of Leviticus had also occurred during the first month of celebration. The instructions that God had given for the worship life of the children of Israel in Leviticus had also been carried out during the same month.

These facts are noted to show just how closely the books of Moses are tied together. In fact, the first Hebrew word in the book of Numbers has a prefix that could be translated "And then." By using this conjunction Moses was simply continuing the narrative of the book of Leviticus. Between Leviticus and Numbers there should be no more hesitation than we would make in the sentence: "I went to the grocery store. And then I went to the hardware store." That there is a division at all is probably due to limitations on the size of a scroll, not a difference in message or in content.

When the Lord spoke to Moses, his instructions for the census were simple and direct. The responsibility for taking the census was placed on Moses, Aaron and one leader from each of the tribes of Israel. The Lord even designated each tribal leader by name. Though the Scriptures do not give us any biographical information about the twelve princes, it is interesting to examine their names. Many of these names indicate a clear reference to God. Note the syllables: El (meaning "God"), Eli ("my God"), Abi ("my father"), Ahi ("my brother").

Elizur	— My God (Eli) the Rock
Shelumiel	— God (El), my Salvation
Elisaph	— My God (Eli) that gathers
Nahshon	— The Diviner
Nethaniel	— God (El), the Giver
Eliab	— My God (Eli), the Father
Elishama	— My God (Eli), the Hearer
Gamaliel	— God (El), the Rewarder
Abidan	— My Father (Abi), is Judge
Ahiezer	— My Brother is Help
Pagiel	— My fate is God (El) or My Prayer-God
Ahira	— My Brother is a Friend

The Lord had designated the workers! The work, however, presents some problems because no single English word describes their duties. Translators vacillate between "census" and "mustering." Since a count was taken, census seems appropriate. Yet since the count included only men twenty or more years old who were able to go to war, the military term "muster" could very appropriately be used.

The procedure for the mustering was defined by four terms: tribe, clan, family, name. The broadest term was "tribe." The tribes of Israel took their names from the twelve sons of Jacob, who had lived about four centuries earlier. Thus there was: the tribe of Simeon, the tribe of Judah, the tribe of Dan, and so on.

Within the tribe there were "clans." The names of the clans were derived from the names of the grandsons of Jacob. For example: Simeon had four sons. Therefore within the tribe of Simeon there were four clans: Hanochite, Palluite, Hezronite and Carmite (Numbers 26:5-6).

The next term, "family," jumps across the centuries to the time of Moses and includes all the people who were descendants of a common, living ancestor. Such extended families presented themselves as a group for the actual counting. The final term "by name" indicates that the census was to include every single person who met the criteria.

A chart that follows will illustrate these terms:

Tribe — son of Jacob	SIMEON			
Clan — sons of Simeon	Hanoch	Pallu	Hezron	Carmi
		↓	↓	
	(430 years in Egypt intervened)			
Family — living people	↓		↓	
	↓	↓	↓	↓
By name **G** Grandfathers	G	G	G	G	G
By name **F** Fathers	F F F F F F F F F F			
By name **S** Sons	SSSSSSSSSSSSSSSSSSSSS			

Since all the children of Israel lived in a single camp, this procedure was both efficient and exact. The oldest man of each of the families could present himself before the census takers. The family head could then define the family tree by reciting his own name and then the names of his sons and grandsons. Looking to the left and right each family leader could determine whether his own brothers and cousins were present and accounted for. By this procedure an accurate count was provided and was even checked and cross-checked in a single day.

The Census Itself

17Moses and Aaron took these men whose names had been given, 18and they called the whole community together on the first day of the second month. The people indicated their ancestry by their clans and families, and the men twenty years old or more were listed by name, one by one, 19as the LORD commanded Moses. And so he counted them in the Desert of Sinai:

20From the descendants of Reuben the firstborn son of Israel: All the men twenty years old or more who were able to serve in the army were listed by name, one by one, according to the records of their clans and families. 21The number from the tribe of Reuben was 46,500.

22From the descendants of Simeon: All the men twenty years old or more who were able to serve in the army were counted and listed by name, one by one, according to the records of their clans and families. 23The number from the tribe of Simeon was 59,300.

24From the descendants of Gad: All the men twenty years old or more who were able to serve in the army were listed by name, according to the records of their clans and families. 25The number from the tribe of Gad was 45,650.

26From the descendants of Judah: All the men twenty years old or more who were able to serve in the army were listed by name, according to the records of their clans and families. 27The number from the tribe of Judah was 74,600.

28From the descendants of Issachar: All the men twenty years old or more who were able to serve in the army were listed by name, according to the records of their clans and families. 29The number from the tribe of Issachar was 54,400.

30 From the descendants of Zebulun:

All the men twenty years old or more who were able to serve in the army were listed by name, according to the records of their clans and families. 31 The number from the tribe of Zebulun was 57,400.

32 From the sons of Joseph:

From the descendants of Ephraim:

All the men twenty years old or more who were able to serve in the army were listed by name, according to the records of their clans and families. 33 The number from the tribe of Ephraim was 40,500.

34 From the descendants of Manasseh:

All the men twenty years old or more who were able to serve in the army were listed by name, according to the records of their clans and families. 35 The number from the tribe of Manasseh was 32,200.

36 From the descendants of Benjamin:

All the men twenty years old or more who were able to serve in the army were listed by name, according to the records of their clans and families. 37 The number from the tribe of Benjamin was 35,400.

38 From the descendants of Dan:

All the men twenty years old or more who were able to serve in the army were listed by name, according to the records of their clans and families. 39 The number from the tribe of Dan was 62,700.

40 From the descendants of Asher:

All the men twenty years old or more who were able to serve in the army were listed by name, according to the records of their clans and families. 41 The number from the tribe of Asher was 41,500.

42 From the descendants of Naphtali:

All the men twenty years old or more who were able to serve in the army were listed by name, according to the records of their clans and families. 43 The number from the tribe of Naphtali was 53,400.

⁴⁴These were the men counted by Moses and Aaron and the twelve leaders of Israel, each one representing his family. ⁴⁵All the Israelites twenty years old or more who were able to serve in Israel's army were counted according to their families. ⁴⁶The total number was 603,550.

⁴⁷The families of the tribe of Levi, however, were not counted along with the others. ⁴⁸The LORD had said to Moses: ⁴⁹"You must not count the tribe of Levi or include them in the census of the other Israelites. ⁵⁰Instead, appoint the Levites to be in charge of the tabernacle of the Testimony — over all its furnishings and everything belonging to it. They are to carry the tabernacle and all its furnishings; they are to take care of it and encamp around it. ⁵¹Whenever the tabernacle is to move, the Levites are to take it down, and whenever the tabernacle is to be set up, the Levites shall do it. Anyone else who goes near it shall be put to death. ⁵²The Israelites are to set up their tents by divisions, each man in his own camp under his own standard. ⁵³The Levites, however, are to set up their tents around the tabernacle of the Testimony so that wrath will not fall on the Israelite community. The Levites are to be responsible for the care of the tabernacle of the Testimony."

⁵⁴The Israelites did all this just as the LORD commanded Moses.

Moses and Aaron proceeded to their task immediately. That very same day they summoned the twelve men who had been appointed to help and then proceeded with the census.

At this point we meet for the first time in the book of Numbers a section which seems unnecessarily tedious and repetitious. Yet this very repetitiousness puts the emphasis on the fact that the children of Israel faithfully carried out the Lord's commands. They already had had a number of opportunities to see that the Lord said what he meant and meant what he said. Had he not sent one plague after another upon the Egyptians, as he had said he would? Had he not rescued the children of Israel at the Red Sea in exactly the way he had predicted he would? Had he not revealed himself on Mount Sinai in a way that inspired awe and respect? Had he not just a few days earlier struck down Nadab and Abihu in the Tent of Meeting, because they had not followed his directions precisely? (Leviticus 10:1-7).

The commands of the God of Israel were not to be trifled with! Therefore let it be tedious! When the count was taken in each of the tribes, they obeyed the commands of the Lord in every detail. Those who were counted were twenty years old, were able to serve in the army and were listed by name according to the clan and family. They did it right. They did it the Lord's way. Here is an example that deserves imitation!

The count was completed. The totals were determined for each tribe and for the entire nation.

A quick survey of the totals for each tribe shows that eleven of the numbers end in even hundreds and one ends with fifty. Though it could be acceptable to assume that the numbers were rounded off to the nearest fifty, it is hard to imagine that Moses would have allowed such a lack of precision. In everything else he noted that the children of Israel did exactly as the Lord commanded. Could it really be that they failed to follow as precisely in the determination of the numbers, since each one was to be counted "by name"? It would seem that the numbers are just as precise as the rest of the information that we have about the census. Therefore one explanation is that God in his wisdom chose on this particular day to make the numbers come out to even 50s and 100s for all the tribes of Israel. Support for this is offered in the third chapter of Numbers. At that point the difference of 273 was noted in the census of the Levites and the counting of the first-born of Israel. Under the same type of command from the Lord the precise number was noted. So it is certainly reasonable to assume that the numbers here are just as precise.

Another explanation would focus on the judgments implied by the mustering of men who could go forth to war. Obviously anyone with apparent mental or physical handicaps would immediately be excluded from the count. But there would certainly be many marginal situations. If it is assumed that the mustering was done in groups of fifty, when the last full group of able-bodied soldiers from a tribe was completed, the mustering for the tribe was considered complete. The remainder would be considered unable to go to war. Using this reasoning the numbers would then come out to even 50s and 100s.

When the mustering had been completed, the total number was remarkable. 603,550 men were able to go to war. The Lord had surely kept his promise to Abraham. Indeed, Abraham's descendants had become a great nation (Genesis 12:2). They were becoming as numerous as the stars (Genesis 15:5). When Jacob moved to Egypt, seventy people went with him (Genesis 46:27). At that point the Lord had repeated the promise in the words, "Do not be afraid to go down to Egypt, for I will make you into a great nation there" (Genesis 46:3).

God's faithfulness to his promise to Abraham and Jacob is a theme that is picked up in the first verses of Exodus. After three and one half centuries the Lord's blessing is evident as we are told in Exodus 1:6: "The Israelites were fruitful and multiplied greatly and became exceedingly numerous, so that the land was filled with them." In response to that growth a new king of Egypt stated, "Look, the Israelites have become much too numerous for us" (Exodus 1:10). He feared that the Israelites would rebel. That fear led the Pharaoh to make things difficult for the Israelites. Nevertheless, two verses later the Bible states, "The more they (the children of Israel) were oppressed, the more they multiplied and spread" (Exodus 1:12). To be sure, the king of Egypt had ordered that the male infants should be killed. Yet apparently even that decree was soon set aside, for the Pharaoh's own daughter rescued Moses.

For Bible believing Christians the statement of Scripture that there were 603,550 men is sufficient reason to accept the figure as accurate. On the other hand, there is also reason for drawing together the numbers that the Scriptures do give us to show that the growth of Israel was not unreasonable.

From Exodus 12:40,41 we learn that the time period from Jacob's arrival in Egypt until the day of the departure of the nation under Moses was exactly 430 years. If we are speaking here in terms of thirty year generations, there would be fourteen and one third generations from the time of Jacob to the time of the Exodus. From this it is possible to project that each generation would have had to produce 2.01 living sons to reach over 600,000 by the time of the Exodus. Presumably there would be an equal number of daughters. This would suggest that the average family had four living children. When Jacob migrated to Egypt, there were fifty-six adult sons and grandsons of the patriarch (Genesis 46:8-27). Since three of these children were the sons of Levi, and since the Levites are not included in the current census of the nation, any statistical projection would have to start with fifty-three male descendants of Jacob. The following table shows the possible growth of Jacob's family tree:

Generation	Number
1	53
2	107
3	214
4	430
5	865
6	1,739

Generation	Number
7	3,495
8	7,025
9	14,120
10	28,382
11	57,047
12	114,665
13	230,477
14	463,260
$^1/_3$ generation	617,680

While statistics can be made to say most anything, this table does indicate that it is not unreasonable to accept the report that the census total for the nation was 603,550.

From the census total the conclusion can also be drawn that the total number of people in the camp of Israel was probably more than 2,000,000. One way to estimate such a figure would be to assume that 55% of the men in a nation will be over nineteen years of age. Such an assumption would suggest that the total number of men and boys among the children of Israel was 1,097,363. Doubling that figure to include the women, the total population for the children of Israel would project out at 2,194,727.

How clearly the Lord had blessed the growth of this nation! What a vast host to sustain with manna in the wilderness!

There have been those who have tried to discredit these census figures. Of course, when people make assumptions that challenge the power and faithfulness of God, the numbers in the book of Numbers do seem to present problems. Some have suggested that all the numbers have an extra zero added. Others that the Hebrew word for thousands should be translated "troop leader." According to this theory there would have been forty-six troop leaders and about 500 troops. But this theory fails on two counts:

(1) There is no clear evidence to support the proposed translation, and (2) There is no way that the number of troop leaders and troops in each tribe can be reconciled with the grand total for the nation. Yet these critics boldly consider their theory more reliable than the Bible record!

There is really only one problem that lies behind such objections to the Scriptures: The critics just do not want to believe the Lord. They do not feel that they can trust the Lord in his promises or his blessings. They also fail to give God credit for being able to give accurate information in the Bible or to perform the miracles that have been recorded in the Scriptures.

Just as little as the Pharaoh was able to stop the growth of the Jewish nation, just so little have the critics of modern times succeeded in discrediting the Scriptures. So when the numbers are taken at face value, the purposes of the Lord become clear. One such purpose was to show how great this nation had become as witnessed by the census. The promises to Abraham had been kept.

A second purpose was to make the children of Israel acutely aware of the fact that with an almighty hand the Lord was providing food for a multitude of people in the wilderness. When a person tries to envision how many truckloads of food are distributed each day in a large city, then the miraculous bounty of the Lord becomes clearly evident because he provided manna for the children of Israel each day of their stay in the wilderness of Sinai. How great and mighty is the Lord! He can give the necessary daily bread, even in a wilderness.

A third purpose of the census was organizing the children of Israel for the battles that were still coming. The lines of command were really very simple. It started from the elders of each tribe and moved down through the family tree till it reached each individual man in the camp. In this way the Lord arranged for this nation to be the instrument through which he would punish the people of Canaan for their sinfulness.

From our vantage point it is easy to see that God also had a hidden purpose. He who knows the end from the beginning knew that it would be vital for the children of Israel to have a precise list of the men who were twenty years old when the people crossed the Red Sea. A generation later that list was consulted at the banks of the Jordan River to determine that every man of the rebellious generation had died in the wilderness. Except for Caleb and Joshua none of the men counted in this census were alive to enter the Promised Land.

On the other hand, a more immediate purpose for the census was to provide order for the camp and the march.

In examining God's purposes it is very evident that he is a God of order (1 Corinthians 14:40). It pleases him greatly if matters pertaining to his people and his service are carried out in an orderly way.

In connection with the census the Lord chose to organize the camp according to his will. As a God of order, he directed that each of the twelve tribes should have an assigned place in the camp. (The Levites, about whom we will hear more in chapter 3, were to be separate from the other tribes.) Within the area of each tribe the individual clans and families would also have clearly designated places. Such order would minimize the bickering and arguments as the children of Israel moved from campsite to campsite in the years that followed.

A simple diagram may help us to visualize the information of this chapter.

⊠ The Tent of Meeting

✕ Tents of Moses, Aaron, Eleazar and Ithamar

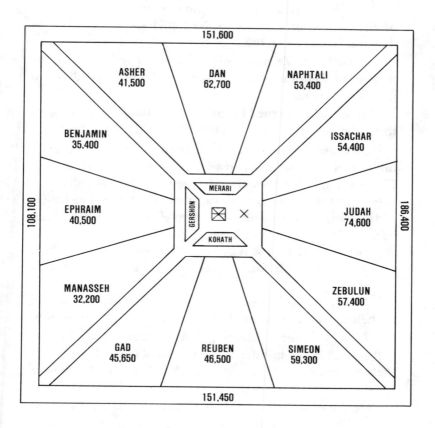

Diagram of the Camp

The Arrangement of the Tribal Camps

2 The LORD said to Moses and Aaron: ²"The Israelites are to camp around the Tent of Meeting some distance from it, each man under his standard with the banners of his family."

³On the east, toward the sunrise, the divisions of the camp of Judah are to encamp under their standard. The leader of the people of Judah is Nahshon son of Amminadab. ⁴His division numbers 74,600.

⁵The tribe of Issachar will camp next to them. The leader of the people of Issachar is Nethanel son of Zuar. ⁶His division numbers 54,400.

⁷The tribe of Zebulun will be next. The leader of the people of Zebulun is Eliab son of Helon. ⁸His division numbers 57,400.

⁹All the men assigned to the camp of Judah, according to their divisions, number 186,400. They will set out first.

¹⁰On the south will be the divisions of the camp of Reuben under their standard. The leader of the people of Reuben is Elizur son of Shedeur. ¹¹His division numbers 46,500.

¹²The tribe of Simeon will camp next to them. The leader of the people of Simeon is Shelumiel son of Zurishaddai. ¹³His division numbers 59,300.

¹⁴The tribe of Gad will be next. The leader of the people of Gad is Eliasaph son of Deuel. ¹⁵His division numbers 45,650.

¹⁶All the men assigned to the camp of Reuben, according to their divisions, number 151,450. They will set out second.

¹⁷Then the Tent of Meeting and the camp of the Levites will set out in the middle of the camps. They will set out in the same order as they encamp, each in his own place under his standard.

¹⁸On the west will be the divisions of the camp of Ephraim under their standard. The leader of the people of Ephraim is Elishama son of Ammihud. ¹⁹His division numbers 40,500.

²⁰The tribe of Manasseh will be next to them. The leader of the people of Manasseh is Gamaliel son of Pedahzur. ²¹His division numbers 32,200.

²²The tribe of Benjamin will be next. The leader of the people of Benjamin is Abidan son of Gideoni. ²³His division numbers 35,400.

²⁴All the men assigned to the camp of Ephraim, according to their divisions, number 108,100. They will set out third.

²⁵On the north will be the divisions of the camp of Dan, under their standard. The leader of the people of Dan is Ahiezer son of Ammishaddai. ²⁶His division numbers 62,700.

²⁷The tribe of Asher will camp next to them. The leader of the people of Asher is Pagiel son of Ocran. ²⁸His division numbers 41,500.

²⁹The tribe of Naphtali will be next. The leader of the people of Naphtali is Ahira son of Enan. ³⁰His division numbers 53,400.

³¹All the men assigned to the camp of Dan number 157,600. They will set out last, under their standards.

³²These are the Israelites, counted according to their families. All those in the camps, by their divisions, number 603,550. ³³The Levites, however, were not counted along with the other Israelites, as the LORD commanded Moses.

³⁴So the Israelites did everything the LORD commanded Moses; that is the way they encamped under their standards, and that is the way they set out, each with his clan and family.

In examining the diagram and the text it is immediately evident that the twelve tribes are divided into four divisions with three tribes in each division. In examining the positions of the four divisions it is noteworthy that Judah has the position of leadership and honor on the east. That position had been determined by God in the parting benediction that Jacob had given his son, Judah (Gensis 49:8-12). In that blessing Jacob had prophesied that Judah would indeed prosper and would be the forefather of the Savior, the Lion from the tribe of Judah.

Anticipating some later events, it is also interesting to note that the tribe of Reuben is located beside the clan of Kohathites. This closeness was later a factor in a rebellious plot against Moses and Aaron (Numbers 16).

In visualizing the camp it seems that at the innermost point of each of the tribal camps the leader of the tribe would erect his tent beside the standard or divisional flag of the tribe. Then the various families would arrange themselves in order in ever widening arcs. Individual families would also have their particular banners (see verse 2) to make it easier for a person to find his way around the camp.

How efficient the arrangement also was for communication: Moses could call the leaders together from the inner circle. He would give them the message. They in turn would pass the word to the various families until it reached the outermost edges of the camp.

How clear the sense of nation and tribe must have been! The people had no problem in defining their roots, since on a daily basis they saw all the tribal flags and family banners arranged in ever-widening arcs around the Tent of Meeting.

The design of the camp also clearly showed God's intention for the nation! The camp faced inward toward the Tent of Meeting; it consciously gathered around the place where the glory of the Lord visibly showed its presence. Flowing outward from the Tent of Meeting was the strength and guidance that the Lord provided. Looking inward the camp was designed to focus the religious life of the people toward the Tent of Meeting. In other words the whole scene showed that their lives were to be focused on the Tent of Meeting and the gracious God who was present there.

The symbolism of God's plan for the camp is obvious: Worship was to be absolutely central in their entire life. Fellowship with God was to be the privilege of his people; the service of God, their delight.

Another part of keeping order was designating the order in which the various divisions were to set out.

Judah, together with the other two tribes in that division, made up the largest group of the Israelites. This group was to set out as a vanguard. Following in turn would come the divisions with Reuben and Ephraim. As a rearguard came the group with the tribe of Dan. The three tribes in this last division made up the second largest group, and so it was appropriate that they should be the rearguard while the nation was on the march.

Truly God is a God of order and wisdom. The children of Israel did exactly as the Lord commanded (verse 34).

The Levites

3 **This is the account of the family of Aaron and Moses at the time the LORD talked with Moses on Mount Sinai.**

²The names of the sons of Aaron were Nadab the firstborn and Abihu, Eleazar and Ithamar. ³Those were the names of Aaron's sons, the anointed priests, who were ordained to serve as priests. ⁴Nadab and Abihu, however, fell dead before the LORD when they made an offering with unauthorized fire before him in the Desert of Sinai. They had no sons; so only Eleazar and Ithamar served as priests during the lifetime of their father Aaron.

The Levites had not been included in the military census, because God had designated them to serve the Lord directly. They enjoyed this high honor because they had rallied to support Moses and had punished the people who worshipped the golden calf.

So the Lord had not forgotten the Levites. He had special responsibilities for them. As the narrative now shifts to the

Levites, a natural starting place is to focus on the two men of the tribe who according to God's plan were most outstanding: Moses and Aaron.

Moses, of course, was the great leader of the children of Israel and the great type of Christ. (See the comments in the introduction.) Yet at this point nothing further is said about Moses because he did not pass any office to his sons. Indeed, his sons are not even listed.

On the other hand, the great work of the High Priest was to be passed on to Aaron's children. Therefore his four sons are mentioned. Through them the priesthood was to be passed on from one generation to another.

But only two of Aaron's sons did actually carry on the priesthood. The other two, Nadab and Abihu, had died in the tabernacle twenty days before the events recorded in this chapter. On the day of their ordination they had brought God's wrath upon themselves by doing their own thing in the sanctuary. They erred because they brought "unauthorized fire" into the sanctuary and used it for the sacrifices. The Lord struck them down immediately. See Exodus 9 for more details. Numbers 4 recalls the unhappy incident and records that Nadab and Abihu died without any sons.

And so the priesthood would pass down through Aaron's surviving sons, Eleazar and Ithamar. The duties of the priesthood in relation to the sacrifices were presented in the first eight chapters of Leviticus. At this point Moses details their responsibilities in relation to the other Levites and the care of the tabernacle.

The Levites Belong Wholly to the Lord

5The LORD said to Moses, 6"Bring the tribe of Levi and present them to Aaron the priest to assist him. 7They are to perform duties for him and for the whole community at the Tent of Meeting by doing the work of the tabernacle. 8They are to take care of all the furnishings of the Tent of Meeting, fulfilling the obligations of the

Israelites by doing the work of the tabernacle. ⁹Give the Levites to Aaron and his sons; they are the Israelites who are to be given wholly to him. ¹⁰Appoint Aaron and his sons to serve as priests; anyone else who approaches the sanctuary must be put to death."

¹¹The LORD also said to Moses, ¹²"I have taken the Levites from among the Israelites in place of the first male offspring of every Israelite woman. The Levites are mine, ¹³for all the firstborn are mine. When I struck down all the firstborn in Egypt, I set apart for myself every firstborn in Israel, whether man or animal. They are to be mine. I am the LORD."

These paragraphs give the broad outline of the position of the Levites in God's plan. They were to belong wholly to the Lord. The entire tribe was consecrated to perform special functions at the Tent of Meeting. Though their work was in and around the Tent of Meeting, they were not priests. Instead they were to serve under the priests, and especially under Aaron, the High Priest, and his successors.

To symbolize this relationship, Moses was directed to present the Levites before Aaron. By this formal presentation the focus of the work and the relationship of the Levites to Aaron and the Lord was to be made clear to all.

As a broad definition of their duties, the Lord indicates that they were to take care of the furnishings of the sanctuary and were to perform a number of duties on behalf of the Israelites. By assigning these duties to the Levites the Lord assured that proper training and care would be observed in connection with the worship activities in the sanctuary. Such preparation was necessary since a person would be put to death for improper actions at the Tent of Meeting. The assignments of the Levites were so important in the eyes of the Lord that there were to be no substitutes for the Levites.

This census brings together two events that had happened to the children of Israel in the preceding year. The first of these events was the great Passover on the night that the Israelites were released from Egypt. On that occasion, except in those homes where the blood of a lamb had been smeared on the doorframes of the home, the Lord had killed all the firstborn in Egypt. On that night the Lord consecrated to himself all the firstborn of the Israelites, because in his mercy the angel of death had passed over them. It was his intention that the firstborn in all generations and in all families belonged to him and should serve him in the tabernacle.

The second event occurred in connection with the idolatrous worship of the golden calf. When Moses had come down from the mountain after forty days, he appealed to the people to punish the idolaters. At that point the Levites were especially zealous in killing those who had worshipped the golden calf (See Exodus 32:25ff for more details). In recognition of the Levites' loyalty, God determined that he would consecrate the Levites to serve in the tabernacle in place of the firstborn sons. In acknowledgement of this arrangement all parents were to bring sacrifices to redeem their firstborn sons.

In the New Testament we are acquainted with the sacrifice for the firstborn son through the actions of Mary and Joseph. They brought this prescribed sacrifice when Jesus was born. In careful obedience Mary and Joseph presented Jesus at the temple and offered two turtledoves as the redemptive sacrifice on behalf of Jesus (Luke 2:22-24).

As the LORD claims the firstborn sons and the Levites he says: "The firstborn sons are mine. The Levites are mine. I am the LORD."

Note that this is one of many occasions in which all four letters of the word "LORD" are capitalized in the English text. Editors use this device to show that the Hebrew text at this point uses the name that the Lord chose for himself when he spoke to Moses at the burning bush. The name God chose had four consonants: JHVH or JHWH. Some translations transliterate those consonants in the words "Jehovah" or "Jahweh." Our translation acknowledges the use of God's self-chosen name by capitalizing all four of the letters in the word LORD. Far more important than the spelling or form of the name in English is the proclamation that the LORD made about his name in Exodus 34:5-7. At that time while Moses was hidden in a cleft in a rock, God indicated that he wanted to be known first and foremost as the God of free and faithful grace. He gladly forgives wickedness and rebellion and sin. Yet when human beings scorn his gospel he will surely punish.

Since the foregoing thoughts are to be included with God's name, we do well to note each time that this name occurs. In the current situation we note that it is the LORD, the compassionate and gracious God, who lays claim to the firstborn sons in Israel. He had spared them at the time of the Passover in Egypt. As the same LORD who is showing mercy to thousands, he chose to give the Levites the high honor of serving in the Tent of Meeting, performing many specified functions directly in his service.

Yet it is the same LORD who will not leave the impenitent sinners unpunished. Only a few days earlier the LORD had struck down Nadab and Abihu. Clearly those who were to serve in the tabernacle could be expected to act in respectful awe before him. This holy and gracious LORD was the one who had separated the Levites for their holy calling. In all seriousness he asserted his purpose by saying, "I am the LORD."

Census: Levites on Behalf of the Firstborn

¹⁴The LORD said to Moses in the Desert of Sinai, ¹⁵"Count the Levites by their families and clans. Count every male a month old

or more." ¹⁶So Moses counted them, as he was commanded by the word of the LORD.

¹⁷These were the names of the sons of Levi:

Gershon, Kohath and Merari.

¹⁸These were the names of the Gershonite clans:

Libni and Shimei.

¹⁹The Kohathite clans:

Amram, Izhar, Hebron and Uzziel.

²⁰The Merarite clans:

Mahli and Mushi.

These were the Levite clans, according to their families.

²¹To Gershon belonged the clans of the Libnites and Shimeites; these were the Gershonite clans. ²²The number of all the males a month old or more who were counted was 7,500. ²³The Gershonite clans were to camp on the west, behind the tabernacle. ²⁴The leader of the families of the Gershonites was Eliasaph son of Lael. ²⁵At the Tent of Meeting the Gershonites were responsible for the care of the tabernacle and tent, its coverings, the curtain at the entrance to the Tent of Meeting, ²⁶the curtains of the courtyard, the curtain at the entrance to the courtyard surrounding the tabernacle and altar, and the ropes — and everything related to their use.

²⁷To Kohath belonged the clans of the Amramites, Izharites, Hebronites and Uzzielites; these were the Kohathite clans. ²⁸The number of all the males a month old or more was 8,600. The Kohathites were responsible for the care of the sanctuary. ²⁹The Kohathite clans were to camp on the south side of the tabernacle. ³⁰The leader of the families of the Kohathites was Elizaphan son of Uzziel. ³¹They were responsible for the care of the ark, the table, the lampstand, the altars, the articles of the sanctuary used in ministering, the curtain, and everything related to their use. ³²The chief leader of the Levites was Eleazar son of Aaron, the priest. He was appointed over those who were responsible for the care of the sanctuary.

³³To Merari belonged the clans of the Mahlites and the Mushites; these were the Merarite clans. ³⁴The number of all the

males a month old or more who were counted was 6,200. ³⁵The leader of the families of the Merarite clans was Zuriel son of Abihail; they were to camp on the north side of the tabernacle. ³⁶The Merarites were appointed to take care of the frames of the tabernacle, its crossbars, posts, bases, all its equipment, and everything related to their use, ³⁷as well as the posts of the surrounding courtyard with their bases, tent pegs and ropes.

³⁸Moses and Aaron and his sons were to camp to the east of the tabernacle, toward the sunrise, in front of the Tent of Meeting. They were responsible for the care of the sanctuary on behalf of the Israelites. Anyone else who approached the sanctuary was to be put to death.

³⁹The total number of Levites counted at the LORD's command by Moses and Aaron according to their clans, including every male a month old or more, was 22,000.

⁴⁰The LORD said to Moses, "Count all the firstborn Israelite males who are a month old or more and make a list of their names. ⁴¹Take the Levites for me in place of all the firstborn of the Israelites, and the livestock of the Levites in place of all the firstborn of the livestock of the Israelites. I am the LORD."

⁴²So Moses counted all the firstborn of the Israelites, as the LORD commanded him. ⁴³The total number of firstborn males a month old or more, listed by name, was 22,273.

⁴⁴The LORD said to Moses, ⁴⁵"Take the Levites in place of all the firstborn of Israel, and the livestock of the Levites in place of their livestock. The Levites are to be mine. I am the LORD. ⁴⁶To redeem the 273 firstborn Israelites who exceed the number of the Levites, ⁴⁷collect five shekels for each one, according to the sanctuary shekel, which weighs twenty gerahs. ⁴⁸Give the money for the redemption of the additional Israelites to Aaron and his sons."

⁴⁹So Moses collected the redemption money from those who exceeded the number redeemed by the Levites. ⁵⁰From the firstborn of the Israelites he collected silver weighing 1,365 shekels, according to the sanctuary shekel. ⁵¹Moses gave the redemption money to Aaron and his sons, as he was commanded by the word of the LORD.

The census of the Levites had different guidelines than the census for the rest of Israel. Among the Levites not only the men of military age but all males a month old and upward were to be counted. Such a guideline was appropriate since the Levites were to be offered in exchange for all the first-born among the Israelites.

As the Levite clans were counted, the total number was reported first. Then Moses added information about the place that each clan had within the camp, about the designated leader, and about the special responsibilities of each clan and about the priest to whom each clan was responsible.

Since Moses and Aaron also belonged to the Levites, the position of their campsites is also reported. Their tents were to be placed on the east side of the tabernacle, facing its entrance, so that they could easily carry out their special functions.

The Gershonites were assigned to care for the tent of the tabernacle itself. This assignment included the exterior curtains of the main entrance, the curtains around the courtyard and all the related equipment. The Kohathites were responsible for the furnishings that stood within the sanctuary itself, for example, the altars, the curtain for the Most Holy Place and any related equipment. The Merarites were responsible for the heavy planks and crosspieces that formed a framework both for the tabernacle and for the courtyard fence, plus all the related equipment.

Yet the focus of this section is on the total number of the Levites. We note again that the number is very reasonable if we assume that in each generation each family on the average produced two living sons, who in turn produced two sons. Starting with the three sons of Levi who came to Egypt with Jacob 430 years earlier, the projection comes out to just over 22,000 Levites that were a month old or more.

But more important, the Levites were to be taken in exchange for the firstborn sons among the children of Israel. So the firstborn sons were also counted. The results were remarkably close: 22,000 Levites; 22,273 firstborn sons. Here we note that the counting of the firstborn is not a round number and adds support to the conclusion that all the numbers are to be taken exactly as they stand. At any rate, there were 273 extra firstborn sons. The Lord determined that they were to be redeemed. The redemption price came to five shekels per person.

On the number of firstborn sons it should be noted that the number here presented would probably have to be those children that were born after the Passover in Egypt, otherwise the number is far too low. Strictly speaking, those were the only ones who really were under the arrangement in which firstborn sons were to be presented as workers at the tabernacle of the Lord.

Even the cattle of the Levites was to be considered a redemption price for the firstborn cattle of all the rest of the Israelites.

The Kohathites

4 The LORD said to Moses and Aaron: ²"Take a census of the Kohathite branch of the Levites by their clans and families. ³Count all the men from thirty to fifty years of age who come to serve in the work in the Tent of Meeting.

⁴"This is the work of the Kohathites in the Tent of Meeting: the care of the most holy things. ⁵When the camp is to move, Aaron and his sons are to go in and take down the shielding curtain and cover the ark of the Testimony with it. ⁶Then they are to cover this with hides of sea cows, spread a cloth of solid blue over that and put the poles in place.

⁷"Over the table of the Presence they are to spread a blue cloth and put on it the plates, dishes and bowls, and the jars for drink

offerings; the bread that is continually there is to remain on it. ⁸Over these they are to spread a scarlet cloth, cover that with hides of sea cows and put its poles in place.

⁹"They are to take a blue cloth and cover the lampstand that is for light, together with its lamps, its wick trimmers and trays, and all its jars for the oil used to supply it. ¹⁰Then they are to wrap it and all its accessories in a covering of hides of sea cows and put it on a carrying frame.

¹¹"Over the gold altar they are to spread a blue cloth and cover that with hides of sea cows and put its poles in place.

¹²"They are to take all the articles used for ministering in the sanctuary, wrap them in a blue cloth, cover that with hides of sea cows and put them on a carrying frame.

¹³"They are to remove the ashes from the bronze altar and spread a purple cloth over it. ¹⁴Then they are to place on it all the utensils used for ministering at the altar, including the firepans, meat forks, shovels and sprinkling bowls. Over it they are to spread a covering of hides of sea cows and put its poles in place.

¹⁵"After Aaron and his sons have finished covering the holy furnishings and all the holy articles, and when the camp is ready to move, the Kohathites are to come to do the carrying. But they must not touch the holy things or they will die. The Kohathites are to carry those things that are in the Tent of Meeting.

¹⁶"Eleazar son of Aaron, the priest, is to have charge of the oil for the light, the fragrant incense, the regular grain offering and the anointing oil. He is to be in charge of the entire tabernacle and everything in it, including its holy furnishings and articles."

¹⁷The LORD said to Moses and Aaron, ¹⁸"See that the Kohathite tribal clans are not cut off from the Levites. ¹⁹So that they may live and not die when they come near the most holy things, do this for them: Aaron and his sons are to go into the sanctuary and assign to each man his work and what he is to carry. ²⁰But the Kohathites must not go in to look at the holy things, even for a moment, or they will die."

At the time the Lord directed Moses to count the Levites, he also defined the responsibilities that each of the three

Levite clans was to have. The Lord also defined certain responsibilities of the priests, who were also of the tribe of Levi. The work of each clan is divided into two broad categories: (1) the tasks involved in the Israelites' worship and (2) the tasks involved in carrying the tabernacle from place to place during the years of wandering. It is interesting to note that only men in the prime of life were to participate in the work of the Levites. Mature enough at thirty and still strong enough till fifty, the Levites carried out their service in the very presence of the Lord.

The work of the Kohathites is described first. Their responsibilities involved the care of the most holy things. The term "most holy things" designated the utensils and furnishings that were used directly in the worship activities at the Tent of Meeting. The Lord chose to manifest his presence in the Tent of Meeting. He had consecrated the Tent of Meeting and all its furnishings by appearing in a cloud. (See Exodus 40 for details.) Therefore he now defined exactly who was responsible for the furnishings in the Tent of Meeting and outlining both the procedures for care and for carrying.

In dealing with the "most holy things" the work of the Kohathites was subject to the supervision of the priests. Whenever the camp was setting out, therefore the priests would begin the process of dismantling the Tent of Meeting by preparing the furnishings in the Tent of Meeting for travel. First, they would take down the curtain that hung between the Most Holy Place and the Holy Place and use it to cover the ark of the Testimony. After that they would place a covering made of the hides of sea cows over it and another covering that was colored blue. Then they would insert poles in the rings along the side of the ark. With the poles in place the Levites could carry the ark without looking at it or touching it. Similar procedures were followed for the Table of the Presence, the lampstand, the golden altar and the bronze altar. Smaller utensils were placed on carrying frames, which were probably similar to stretchers.

After the priests had covered all the furnishings, the Kohathites were allowed to come in and take the items from the Tent of Meeting. Because these items were the most holy things, the Kohathites were directed to carry them by hand. They were not even allowed to put any of these items on a cart. Further, they were warned that they were not to touch or even look at any of the items even for a moment. To look at the holy things or to touch them meant instant death. Careful, detailed planning and instruction of each of the Kohathites was ordered by the Lord. Though he would surely punish disobedience or carelessness by death, he did not wish to dispense death to people who didn't know what they were doing.

What a solemn warning here for those who deal with God's holy things at any time! In the New Testament the holy thing is the message of reconciliation based on a redemption earned by the Savior. That message must be undefiled! Indeed what that message deserves in reverence can not be transferred to the parts or equipment of our churches. As respectful as we might choose to be with the communion ware or in front of the altar, the function of all things is to point us to the Word of God, which is the holy thing of the New Testament.

The work of the Kohathites was under the supervision of Eleazar, the priest, the son of Aaron. Eleazar had the additional responsibilities of caring for the "oil for the light, the fragrant incense, the regular grain offering and the anointing oil."

The Gershonites

²¹The LORD said to Moses, ²²"Take a census also of the Gershonites by their families and clans. ²³Count all the men from thirty to fifty years of age who come to serve in the work at the Tent of Meeting.

²⁴"This is the service of the Gershonite clans as they work and carry burdens: ²⁵They are to carry the curtains of the tabernacle, the Tent of Meeting, its covering and the outer covering of hides of sea cows, the curtains for the entrance to the Tent of Meeting, ²⁶the curtains of the courtyard surrounding the tabernacle and altar, the curtain for the entrance, the ropes and all the equipment used in its service. The Gershonites are to do all that needs to be done with these things. ²⁷All their service, whether carrying or doing other work, is to be done under the direction of Aaron and his sons. You shall assign to them as their responsibility all they are to carry. ²⁸This is the service of the Gershonite clans at the Tent of Meeting. Their duties are to be under the direction of Ithamar son of Aaron, the priest."

After the Kohathites had removed the consecrated equipment, the Gershonites were to come and carry all the items that were made of cloth — the Tent of Meeting itself plus all the curtains that surrounded the court around the Tent of Meeting. This material was bulky, but relatively not very heavy. A little later we will see that provisions were made for a wagon on which to carry these materials.

The Merarites

²⁹"Count the Merarites by their clans and families. ³⁰Count all the men from thirty to fifty years of age who come to serve in the work at the Tent of Meeting. ³¹This is their duty as they perform service at the Tent of Meeting: to carry the frames of the tabernacle, its crossbars, posts and bases, ³²as well as the posts of the surrounding courtyard with their bases, tent pegs, ropes, all their

equipment and everything related to their use. Assign to each man the specific things he is to carry. ³³This is the service of the Merarite clans as they work at the Tent of Meeting under the direction of Ithamar son of Aaron, the priest."

The work of the Merarites was to move the wooden framework that supported both the Tent of Meeting and the curtains that surrounded the courtyard. The wood and metal were bulky and heavy. We will again note later that several wagons were provided for carrying these items.

The work of the Gershonites and the Merarites was under the supervision of Ithamar, who was also a priest and son of Aaron.

As the Lord gave specific instructions to each Levite clan, he also commanded that each person was to be assigned a particular function. Each Levite was to be so thoroughly instructed that he could do his work precisely. Such care was vital. Any error would result in death.

Define the work. Give careful instructions. Expect that the work will be done as instructed — following such basic management principles the Lord was truly showing his concern that a minimal number of errors would occur.

The Numbering of the Levites for the Work in the Tent

³⁴Moses, Aaron and the leaders of the community counted the Kohathites by their clans and families. ³⁵All the men from thirty to fifty years of age who came to serve in the work in the Tent of Meeting, ³⁶counted by clans, were 2,750. ³⁷This was the total of all those in the Kohathite clans who served in the Tent of Meeting. Moses and Aaron counted them according to the Lord's command through Moses.

³⁸The Gershonites were counted by their clans and families. ³⁹All the men from thirty to fifty years of age who came to serve in the work at the Tent of Meeting, ⁴⁰counted by their clans and

families, were 2,630. [41]This was the total of all those in the Gershonite clans who served at the Tent of Meeting. Moses and Aaron counted them according to the LORD's command.

[42]The Merarites were counted by their clans and families. [43]All the men from thirty to fifty years of age who came to serve in the work at the Tent of Meeting, [44]counted by their clans, were 3,200. [45]This was the total of all those in the Merarite clans. Moses and Aaron counted them according to the LORD's command through Moses.

[46]So Moses, Aaron and the leaders of Israel counted all the Levites by their clans and families. [47]All the men from thirty to fifty years of age who came to do the work of serving and carrying the Tent of Meeting [48]numbered 8,580. [49]At the LORD's command through Moses, each was assigned his work and told what to carry.

Thus they were counted, as the LORD commanded Moses.

The purpose of this census was to determine the people who would actually serve in the Tent of Meeting. There were 8,580 Levites between the ages of thirty and fifty. Obviously it was not necessary for each Levite to serve every day. By taking turns they were able to share the duties, so they did not become really burdensome. Certainly there must also have been some cooperation so that those who had the duty of carrying the tabernacle and its furnishings would have help on that day in moving their own families.

The Lord had indicated that the work of the Levites involved very serious responsibilities. Therefore he also limited the officiants to those who were in the prime of life. By the time they were thirty they would be mature enough to avoid careless errors. Until the time they were fifty they would have the required physical strength.

What high honor the Lord gave the Levites! It was their privilege to serve within the tabernacle directly under the priest. They were responsible for transporting the Tent of

Meeting! To be sure, the high honor also meant that some days the men had to arrange with friends and neighbors to get their families moved. Yet they apparently found hands willing and able to help!

With high honor came great responsibility as well. The Levites had to handle the furnishings of the Tabernacle carefully, precisely as the Lord had commanded. If they failed to do so, the penalty was death — a penalty that God could and would mete out.

How clearly the Lord showed that it is important for those who serve before him in the public ministry to train themselves well, so that they truly do as he wishes. On the other hand, let man always come before the Lord with awe and respect. There is no one higher, none greater, none more powerful. Yet there is also none more gracious, kind and good. Serve him! Serve him well!

The Levites were told exactly what their individual duties were; from that moment on they knew automatically what was expected of them. Such a wise distribution of burdens is to be recommended to this day in the church of Christ; it makes for better work in the Lord's vineyard.

FROM SINAI TO KADESH

Life as Individuals

In chapters five and six God turns his attention to matters that affected the individuals in the camp of the Israelites. The regulations regarding ceremonial uncleanness had already been dealt with in Leviticus. At this point the Lord directed that the camp should be cleansed. In the law of jealousy the Lord addressed the possibility that very significant strife could come into the camp if jealousy would be allowed to fester. The first part of chapter six defines a number of regulations about those who chose to make voluntary vows. Each of these topics deals with the way in which the individual Israelite was to conduct himself in his personal life.

Purification of the Camp

5 **The LORD said to Moses, ²"Command the Israelites to send away from the camp anyone who has an infectious skin disease or a discharge of any kind, or who is ceremonially unclean because of a dead body. ³Send away male and female alike; send them outside the camp so they will not defile their camp, where I dwell among them." ⁴The Israelites did this; they sent them outside the camp. They did just as the LORD had instructed Moses.**

In Leviticus 13-15 God gave directives regarding the diagnosis of various skin diseases and assorted boils, spots and infections. He had specified that anyone so affected was ceremonially unclean. He had also specified that anyone who had come in contact with a dead body was ceremonially unclean. Ceremonial uncleanness meant that the person had to stay outside the camp, wear torn clothes, cover the lower part of his face and shout, "Unclean! Unclean!" whenever anyone came near. During the time the unclean person was excluded from the camp he could not participate in the worship life or the social life of the camp.

In Numbers the Lord commanded Moses to put those directives into practice and remove those that were unclean from the camp. The reason that they were to be removed from the camp is given in the words, "where I dwell among them." The Lord who is the source of life and light was actually present in Israel's camp and he did not want these examples of disease and death to defile the camp. Three categories of ceremonial uncleanness are listed: those with infectious skin diseases, those with discharges and those who had been in contact with a dead body. At this point they were all excluded from the camp.

The requirement to remove the people from the camp, even temporarily, calls to mind the picture of people who were in fact outcasts. Ceremonial uncleanness comes to our attention frequently during our Savior's ministry, especially in the lepers who appealed to him. When exclusion from society and the church were the consequences of uncleanness we can imagine the urgency in the pleas of the ten lepers (Luke 17:12) and the desperation of the woman who had been bleeding for twelve years (Matthew 9:20). How graciously our Savior acted whenever he healed such outcasts!

When One Person Wrongs Another

5The Lord said to Moses, 6"Say to the Israelites: 'when a man or woman wrongs another in any way and so is unfaithful to the Lord, that person is guilty 7and must confess the sin he has committed. He must make full restitution for his wrong, add one fifth to it and give it all to the person he has wronged. 8But if that

person has no close relative to whom restitution can be made for the wrong, the restitution belongs to the LORD and must be given to the priest, along with the ram with which atonement is made for him. ⁹All the sacred contributions the Israelites bring to a priest will belong to him. ¹⁰Each man's sacred gifts are his own, but what he gives to the priest will belong to the priest.' "

Whenever human beings live together in close contact, there will always be many ways in which they wrong one another. In this paragraph "wrongs" means any type of sin against another person.

When a wrong has been committed, three points were to be considered. The first point is that the wrongdoer is guilty. The guilt cannot be explained away. The next point is that the guilty person is to confess his sin before the Lord. The seriousness of sin is always in the fact that a person has been "unfaithful to the LORD" even though the act has been against some person. Finally, the guilty person is to make full restitution and add one fifth to it.

How clearly the Lord shows that he takes sin seriously! In fact, God takes sin so seriously that he considers every sin as a sin against himself. This is true even though the sin is against some human being. The most serious aspect of sin is that it is an offense against God.

King David recognized this principle very clearly. When the Prophet Nathan led David to confess his sin, the king's response was: "I have sinned against the LORD" (2 Samuel 12:13). This overwhelming sense of guilt before the Lord rose above the sense of guilt in sinning with Bathsheba and against her husband Uriah.

The requirement to add one fifth to the full restitution reminds us of a beautiful example in the New Testament. Jesus had come to the home of a man named Zacchaeus (Luke 19:1-10). Jesus reached Zacchaeus' heart with the gospel. Zacchaeus then showed eagerness to please the Lord. He went beyond the requirement of the Old Testament: he promised to return four times as much to anyone whom he may have cheated and gave half his possessions to the poor. What power there is in the gospel to change hearts!

Through Moses the Lord also addressed an exceptional case. Supposing that a person who has been wronged would not personally be able to receive the restitution (if, for example, the person had died). If there were no living relative who could act on behalf of the wronged person, then the one who had sinned had the responsibility of making restitution through the priest. The items involved in the restitution became the property of the priest together with the ram of atonement that was required. Clearly the Lord's first goal was to provide for restitution to the offended party. Yet in the unusual case the offender was to know that his sin was in essence against the Lord.

The paragraph closes with a general principle: any gifts that a person chooses to bring are really his own until the moment when he chooses to make the sacred gift. Once the decision was made, however, the gift belonged to the priest, as God's representative.

The Law of Jealousy

11 Then the LORD said to Moses, 12"Speak to the Israelites and say to them: 'If a man's wife goes astray and is unfaithful to him 13by sleeping with another man, and this is hidden from her husband and her impurity is undetected (since there is no witness against her and she has not been caught in the act), 14and if feelings of jealousy come over her husband and he suspects his wife and she is impure — or if he is jealous and suspects her even though she is not impure — 15then he is to take his wife to the priest. He must also take an offering of a tenth of an ephah of barley flour on her behalf. He must not pour oil on it or put

incense on it, because it is a grain offering for jealousy, a reminder offering to draw attention to guilt.

16" 'The priest shall bring her and have her stand before the LORD. 17Then he shall take some holy water in a clay jar and put some dust from the tabernacle floor into the water. 18After the priest has had the woman stand before the LORD, he shall loosen her hair and place in her hands the reminder offering, the grain offering for jealousy, while he himself holds the bitter water that brings a curse. 19Then the priest shall put the woman under oath and say to her, "If no other man has slept with you and you have not gone astray and become impure while married to your husband, may this bitter water that brings a curse not harm you. 20But if you have gone astray while married to your husband and you have defiled yourself by sleeping with a man other than your husband" — 21here the priest is to put the woman under this curse of the oath — "may the LORD cause your people to curse and denounce you when he causes your thigh to waste away and your abdomen to swell. 22May this water that brings a curse enter your body so that your abdomen swells and your thigh wastes away."

" 'Then the woman is to say, "Amen. So be it."

23" 'The priest is to write these curses on a scroll and then wash them off into the bitter water. 24He shall have the woman drink the bitter water that brings a curse, and this water will enter her and cause bitter suffering. 25The priest is to take from her hands the grain offering for jealousy, wave it before the LORD and bring it to the altar. 26The priest is then to take a handful of the grain offering as a memorial offering and burn it on the altar; after that, he is to have the woman drink the water. 27If she has defiled herself and been unfaithful to her husband, then when she is made to drink the water that brings a curse, it will go into her and cause bitter suffering; her abdomen will swell and her thigh waste away, and she will become accursed among her people. 28If, however, the woman has not defiled herself and is free from impurity, she will be cleared of guilt and will be able to have children.

29" 'This, then, is the law of jealousy when a woman goes astray and defiles herself while married to her husband, 30or when feelings of jealousy come over a man because he suspects his wife. The priest is to have her stand before the LORD and is to apply this entire law to her. [31] The husband will be innocent of any wrongdoing, but the woman will bear the consequences of her sin.' "

The Lord himself designates this section as the "law of jealousy" (verse 29). Jealousy must be distinguished here from known adultery.

In the Mosaic law the punishment for adultery left no doubt about the seriousness of that sin against God's law. If a person was caught in the act of adultery, God's law provided that both the man and the woman should be executed immediately. There is an example of capital punishment for adultery later in Numbers. Phineas, the priest, executed a couple in the act of adultery, driving his spear through both at once (Numbers 25:6ff.). Adultery is a sin!

At this point God announced a procedure to deal with a husband's feelings of jealousy. Whether his feelings were legitimate or unfounded, God intended that the corrosive feeling be addressed and removed. To understand what follows, it will help to remember that the temporary and unsettled conditions under which the Israelites lived for almost forty years in the desert brought special temptations. When a number of relatives and in-laws, married and unmarried, lived under the same roof, the temptation to adultery was a constant threat. God therefore outlined a plan for a husband who suspected his wife of being unfaithful to him.

Two cases are cited as examples. In the one case a wife has been unfaithful to her husband and he senses this, although he has no proof. In the other case, his feelings of jealousy are very real, but they are merely the result of his own suspicion. There is no basis in fact.

Whether proper or improper, the husband's feelings were very real. To prevent further erosion of the marriage, the husband was directed to bring his wife and an offering before the priest. By doing this he would put the matter before the Lord for judgment.

Two symbolic acts are particularly prominent: the preparation of the bitter water and the solemn oath with its curse.

In connection with the bitter water the priest was to perform two additional solemn acts. First, he was to take some dust from the floor of the tabernacle and mix it with the water. This act was to emphasize the sanctity of the acts that were to follow. The second solemn act was that the oath with its curse was to be written on a scroll and then the writing was to be washed off into the water. This act was to symbolize that the oath would be more than mere words. The curse would actually be real within the woman, whether or not the curse was finally carried out. Only in the case of unfaithfulness, however, would the woman be affected by the curse. Then as her abdomen would swell and her thighs waste away, the adulteress would also forfeit the ability to bear children.

The priest's function was to make the offering, to recite the oath to the woman, to solicit her solemn "Amen. So be it," and to write the curse on the scroll and wash it off.

When the woman had drunk the water, the matter was in the hands of the Lord. Surely the power was with the Lord, not in the materials that were to be used. If after the ritual it became evident that the wife was innocent, the Lord stated very emphatically that she would be able to bear children. On the other hand, if she had indeed been unfaithful, she would bear the results of her sin. Her body would waste away and she would not be able to bear children.

In this unusual section of the Scripture we have additional evidence of how concerned the LORD was to preserve the purity of the people he had chosen as his own. On the one hand, God did not want a jealous husband to endanger the life of a man he suspects of having seduced his wife. Neither, however, did God want his people to be indifferent toward sexual immorality and to tolerate adulterous behavior. It might also be mentioned that an innocent, outraged wife could insist on this public justification of herself, to the humiliation of her husband.

At any rate, the Scriptures do not record a situation in which someone invoked this "law of jealousy."

In the New Testament an arrangement like this is unknown. Yet all Christians will bear in mind the necessity of keeping their sexual life unspotted, whether their status in life is married or unmarried!

Nazirite or Voluntary Vows: The Requirements

6 The Lord said to Moses, **2**"Speak to the Israelites and say to them: 'If a man or woman wants to make a special vow, a vow of separation to the Lord as a Nazirite, **3**he must abstain from wine and other fermented drink and must not drink vinegar made from wine or from other fermented drink. He must not drink grape juice or eat grapes or raisins. **4**As long as he is a Nazirite, he must not eat anything that comes from the grapevine, not even the seeds or skins.

5 'During the entire period of his vow of separation no razor may be used on his head. He must be holy until the period of his separation to the Lord is over; he must let the hair of his head grow long.' "

The Lord spelled out many details of worship for the children of Israel. However, he also gave them an opportunity to express their faith by bringing offerings that were voluntary. One form of voluntary offering was the Nazirite vow.

The word "Nazirite" is related to the Hebrew word for vow. That a Nazirite vow was voluntary is clear from the words: "If a man or woman wants to make a special vow. . . ." There was no requirement to make such vows. But if an Israelite made a vow, certain requirements had to be met. The vow implied that certain, specific commitments had been made.

The first requirement was that the Nazirite abstain from any type of alcoholic beverage. How well the Lord knows human nature! For the Lord makes it very, very clear that he does not want any fooling around with the borderlines between right and wrong. The Nazirite was not even to drink grape juice, to eat raisins or to use any of the by-products of the grape. For this voluntary vow the Lord wanted no toying with the borderline of right and wrong.

The second requirement was that the Nazirite was to use no razor on his head during the entire time involved in the vow. His hair was to be allowed to grow long. His long hair was a testimony to other people that he had made a voluntary vow to the Lord.

Christians are probably most familiar with the Nazirite vow through the history of Samson (Judges 13-16). He was a lifetime Nazirite. He was to let his hair grow long during his entire life. For him the Lord made the special promise that while his hair was uncut, he would be granted great strength. His downfall came when he broke his vow to the Lord, despised his Nazirite status, and Delilah cut his hair.

Nazirite or Voluntary Vow: A Prohibition

6" 'Throughout the period of his separation to the Lord he must not go near a dead body. 7Even if his own father or mother or brother or sister dies, he must not make himself ceremonially unclean on account of them, because the symbol of his separation to God is on his head. 8Throughout the period of his separation he is consecrated to the Lord.

⁹" 'If someone dies suddenly in his presence, thus defiling the hair he has dedicated, he must shave his head on the day of his cleansing — the seventh day. ¹⁰Then on the eighth day he must bring two doves or two young pigeons to the priest at the entrance to the Tent of Meeting. ¹¹The priest is to offer one as a sin offering and the other as a burnt offering to make atonement for him because he sinned by being in the presence of the dead body. That same day he is to consecrate his head. ¹²He must dedicate himself to the LORD for the period of his separation and must bring a year-old male lamb as a guilt offering. The previous days do not count, because he became defiled during his separation.' "

The third requirement for a person who had taken a Nazirite vow was that under no circumstances was he to go near a dead body. This directive superseded even the close ties of family. Because he had consecrated himself to the Lord through his vow, he was to be extremely careful about avoiding any situation that would make him ceremonially unclean through contact with a dead body.

But there was also the possibility that he would be in the presence of someone who died suddenly or unexpectedly. If that happened he would have to shave his head on the seventh day — the day of his purification from the ceremonially uncleanness. On the next day he was to start over again on fulfilling his vow by bringing three offerings. A sin offering (a dove or pigeon) was to be brought to make atonement which would reestablish the covenant with God which had been broken by the contact with a dead body. A burnt offering (again a dove or pigeon) would be the Nazirite's way of rededicating himself totally to the Lord. The third offering was a lamb as a guilt offering, as an atonement for sin.

On the day of cleansing, the person had to start over again to complete the stipulations of his vow. The previous days did not count. He had to start from the beginning.

Nazirite or Voluntary Vow: The Conclusion

¹³" 'Now this is the law for the Nazirite when the period of his separation is over. He is to be brought to the entrance to the Tent of Meeting. ¹⁴There he is to present his offerings to the LORD: a year-old male lamb without defect for a burnt offering, a year-old ewe lamb without defect for a sin offering, a ram without defect for a fellowship offering, ¹⁵together with their grain offerings and drink offerings, and a basket of bread made without yeast — cakes made of fine flour mixed with oil, and wafers spread with oil.

¹⁶" 'The priest is to present them before the LORD and make the sin offering and the burnt offering. ¹⁷He is to present the basket of unleavened bread and is to sacrifice the ram as a fellowship offering to the LORD, together with its grain offering and drink offering.

¹⁸" 'Then at the entrance to the Tent of Meeting, the Nazirite must shave off the hair that he dedicated. He is to take the hair and put it in the fire that is under the sacrifice of the fellowship offering.

¹⁹" 'After the Nazirite has shaved off the hair of his dedication, the priest is to place in his hands a boiled shoulder of the ram, and a cake and a wafer from the basket, both made without yeast. ²⁰The priest shall then wave them before the LORD as a wave offering; they are holy and belong to the priest, together with the breast that was waved and the thigh that was presented. After that, the Nazirite may drink wine.

²¹" 'This is the law of the Nazirite who vows his offering to the LORD in accordance with his separation, in addition to whatever else he can afford. He must fulfill the vow he has made, according to the law of the Nazirite.' "

At the conclusion of his vow the Nazirite was to present himself at the Tent of Meeting and offer three sacrifices. The first was a sin offering. How well the Lord knows the inclinations of the sinful nature! The Nazirite would have just completed a period of days or months or even years in which he had voluntarily been doing something extra in the service of the Lord. Yet at the conclusion of the vow he was not allowed to think that he had attained some special status before the Lord. The sin offering symbolized that death was necessary to pay for sin and the Lord was preparing a Substitute (Jesus) for our sin. How necessary this was because human nature is all too inclined to come before the Lord, saying: "Look, Lord! Look at what I have done!" After the sin offering the Nazirite offered his burnt offering, in token of his total dedication to God.

After the sin offering and burnt offering had been offered by the priest, it was time for the fellowship offering. This offering expressed the worshiper's joy in his fellowship with God. The offerer would join with the priest, who in this case was God's representative to the people, in a fellowship meal which was a celebration of the fellowship that exists between God and the forgiven sinner. How wonderful that restored fellowship is! The animal blood that was shed emphasized again that fellowship rests on the sacrifice for sin. We have good reason to come before the Lord humbly, even at those times when we have done special things in his service!

In connection with the presentation of the fellowship offering the Nazirite was to shave off the hair that he had dedicated to the Lord. The hair was to be placed in the fire under the fellowship offering. This act symbolized that man can perish as easily as the hair is consumed in the fire. The only hope of sinful mankind, is in a fellowship restored on the basis of God's grace. In concluding this section on the Nazirite vows, we note that the vows were voluntary vows. God wanted his people to look upon vows as an opportunity, not a requirement. Yet once the vow was taken there was no way to avoid going all the way in the completion of the vow. At the end of the vow the sacrifices were designed to remind the Nazirite of his unworthiness. The sacrifices

showed exactly the thoughts that are expressed in the
second stanza of the familiar hymn, "Rock of Ages":

> Not the labors of my hands
> > Can fulfill thy law's demands;
> Could my zeal no respite know,
> > Could my tears forever flow,
> All for sin could not atone;
> > Thou must save and thou alone.

FROM SINAI TO KADESH

Life in Worship

A proclamation that the Lord made to Moses reaches across all the centuries to the present. We still use the Aaronic benediction in our church services. God gave it first to the children of Israel for their worship life. Other aspects of their worship life includes the generous offerings that the leaders of each tribe brought at the dedication of the tabernacle and the lamps that were to be inside the sanctuary. As helpers in Israel's worship life the Levites were consecrated to the Lord. Then when one full year had passed since they left Egypt the Israelites celebrated their first commemorative Passover.

The Benediction of the Lord

22The LORD said to Moses, 23"Tell Aaron and his sons, 'This is how you are to bless the Israelites. Say to them:

24" ' "The LORD bless you
    and keep you;
25the LORD make his face shine upon you
    and be gracious to you;
26the LORD turn his face toward you
    and give you peace." '

27"So they will put my name on the Israelites, and I will bless them."

In the worship life of the Israelites the Lord wanted to be known as a gracious and merciful God. Therefore he gave the priests the words of the Aaronic benediction or blessing.

Because the words of this benediction so clearly present God as the God of free and faithful grace, this blessing is also gladly used in the New Testament era. As Christians we choose this blessing to close our worship services.

In referring to himself God here uses the special name that he has chosen for himself, and therefore each letter of the word "LORD" is capitalized. Through this name the Lord presents himself to us as the "compassionate and gracious God, slow to anger, abounding in love and faithfulness, maintaining love to thousands, and forgiving wickedness, rebellion and sin" (Exodus 34:9,10). As such a compassionate and gracious God, the Lord reaches out to us to bless us.

Because the word "LORD" is repeated three times, we also perceive a reference to the Trinity. Though we, as creatures, are limited in our ability to probe the depths of the Trinity, we can appreciate the truth that the triune God acts on our behalf. As each of the divine persons carries out his work, the triune God reaches out to bless all those who believe in the Messiah, our Lord Jesus Christ. All three are involved in our salvation.

The first phrase refers especially to the work of God the Father. The blessing from the Father includes all aspects of our life. Wherever we look we can see how the Lord blesses us through the physical, material possessions that he gives us. Luther's explanation to the first Article of the Creed summarizes these blessings very concisely, noting that the Lord "gave me my body and soul, eyes, ears and all my members, my mind and all my abilities," and that he "richly and daily provides clothing and shoes, food and drink, house and home, wife and children, land, cattle and all I own."

We need only look about in our homes! Look at the food and furniture, the children and cars, dishes and dresses, the

61

suits and sofas and even the electricity mysteriously present in the wall sockets. Count the many ways in which the Lord blesses us with temporal gifts. Just as surely the Lord blesses us with talents and abilities. With mind and hand we can indeed make a living. With the same mind and hands we can serve him.

Further, our heavenly Father blesses and keeps us as he answers our requests when we pray in the Lord's Prayer, "Lead us not into temptation; but deliver us from evil." How often the Lord keeps us by preventing problems and dangers from overwhelming us! How zealously the Lord works to keep us from going to those places where we will be tempted to sin! Yet, on the other hand, how loving the Lord is when he allows testings to come into our lives, for he promises that he will also make a way of escape and that all things will work together for good to those who love him. Ultimately the richest way in which the Lord blesses us is that he keeps us faithful to the gospel to the end of our lives. It is also his blessing that he will deliver us from this present evil world into the perfection of his glory in heaven. All these blessings the Lord gladly includes in the benediction: "The LORD bless you and keep you."

The second phrase of the benediction addresses the fact that human beings are sinful. By birth man is in rebellion against God. The only hope for such rebels lies in the fact that God is gracious to us. How clearly we see God's love for us in the work of our Redeemer, Jesus Christ. Using Luther's explanation of the Second Article of the Creed, we note that God is gracious to us in Jesus, who "has redeemed me, a lost and condemned creature, purchased and won me from all sins, from death and from the power of the devil, not with gold or silver, but with his holy, precious blood and his innocent suffering and death. All this he did that I should be his own, and live under him in his kingdom, and serve him in everlasting righteousness, innocence and blessedness." That is God's grace — God's undeserved kindness to us. It is grace in Christ. For in Christ God shows his love to us — a deep, profound love which loves us also when we deserve it least because of our sin. In such love God makes his face shine upon us. Just as the face of a proud, new mother radiates love, so God looks at us, covering all our sins with the perfect redemption that Christ has purchased for us. All these blessings the Lord gladly includes in the benediction: "The LORD make his face shine on you and be gracious to you."

In the third phrase of the benediction we see the work of the third person in the Trinity: God the Holy Ghost or Holy Spirit. The phrase "turn his face toward you" indicates that the Lord gladly looks upon each of us as individuals. By contrast, how sad it would be if God would turn his back on any of us, ignore us and leave us to the lot that we deserve. How wonderful this work of the Holy Spirit! He turns rebels into his children by leading them to faith in Christ Jesus! He makes the blind to see by leading them to Christ, the Light of the world. As the Giver of life, he gives life to those who are dead in trespasses and sin. Every believer is a miracle of the Holy Spirit! It is he who has "called me by the gospel, enlightened me with his gifts, sanctified and kept me in the true faith" (Luther's Catechism). In the miracle of conversion the Holy Spirit gives us peace because we know that through Christ we are reconciled to God. We also know with the certainty of faith that as long as we are right with God through Christ, everything in our life will also work out right for us. The believer enjoys a peace that stands up in the fiercest trials — yes even in the face of death. What peace there is to know that whether we live or whether we die we are the Lord's. Anchored in this faith we can exclaim with St. Paul: "Neither death nor life, neither angels nor demons, neither the present nor the future, nor any powers, neither height nor depth, nor anything else in all creation, will be able to separate us from the love of God that is in Christ Jesus our Lord" (Romans 8:38-39). Angels proclaimed this peace at the first Christmas Eve: "Peace on earth, good will to man." Jesus promised the peace from the Holy Spirit when he said, "Peace I leave with you; my peace I give you" (John 14:27). Your pastor prays that you may enjoy this peace each time after the sermon when he uses the words: "And the peace of God, which transcends all understanding, will guard your hearts and your minds in Christ Jesus" (Philippians 4:7).

What marvelous blessings the Lord gives to every believer! His divine power and love stand behind each of the words in the benediction: "So they will put my name on the Israelites, and I will bless them." The name of God was indeed on the Israelites, for in the name Israel is the meaning "man of God." In the New Testament that name is also on us as we claim the name "Christian," which really means that we are followers of Christ. Of such believers the Lord gladly says, "I will bless them." This promise makes the benediction far more than mere words or a pious wish. The Lord stands behind each word. As the triune God he gladly grants these blessings to each of us.

To such a benediction believers in all ages have gladly said, "Amen. So be it."

Amen. So be it! LORD, God the Father, Creator and Preserver, bless and keep us!

Amen. So be it! LORD, Jesus Christ, Savior and Lord, make your face shine upon us and be gracious to us!

Amen. So be it! LORD, Holy Spirit, Sanctifier and Counselor, turn your face toward us and give us peace!

64

Dedication Day Offerings of the Leaders of Israel

7 When Moses finished setting up the tabernacle, he anointed it and consecrated it and all its furnishings. He also anointed and consecrated the altar and all its utensils. ²Then the leaders of Israel, the heads of families who were the tribal leaders in charge of those who were counted, made offerings. ³They brought as their gifts before the Lord six covered carts and twelve oxen — an ox from each leader and a cart from every two. These they presented before the tabernacle.

⁴The Lord said to Moses, ⁵"Accept these from them, that they may be used in the work at the Tent of Meeting. Give them to the Levites as each man's work requires."

⁶So Moses took the carts and oxen and gave them to the Levites. ⁷He gave two carts and four oxen to the Gershonites, as their work required, ⁸and he gave four carts and eight oxen to the Merarites, as their work required. They were all under the direction of Ithamar son of Aaron, the priest. ⁹But Moses did not give any to the Kohathites, because they were to carry on their shoulders the holy things, for which they were responsible.

The first sentence of this section takes us back to the dedication of the tabernacle recorded in Exodus 40. The various events about the census recorded in the first six chapters of Numbers actually occurred about a month after the dedication. On the day of the dedication of the tabernacle the leaders of the Israelites brought special gifts. As the names are presented, the reason Moses reported the census first now begins to make good sense. The leaders identified in the census are the people who represent each tribe in bringing the gifts for the dedication.

On the day of the dedication the leaders of Israel brought six carts and twelve oxen as a gift to the Lord. The Lord instructed Moses to accept the gifts and give them to the Levites for their work in transporting the tabernacle.

The Gershonites who were responsible for the curtains and coverings of the tabernacle were given two carts. The Merarites who had the responsibility for transporting the much heavier and bulkier timbers that formed the framework for the tabernacle were given four carts. No cart was assigned to the Kohathites because they had been specifically instructed to carry all the holy objects on their shoulders.

In this situation as in many situations in the church it is important to see the hand of the Lord. He does open the hearts of his people to provide whatever is necessary. Believers do well to give both the Lord and the givers the credit they deserve.

Twelve Days of Dedication Offerings

10 When the altar was anointed, the leaders brought their offerings for its dedication and presented them before the altar. 11 For the LORD had said to Moses, "Each day one leader is to bring his offering for the dedication of the altar."

12 The one who brought his offering on the first day was Nahshon son of Amminadab of the tribe of Judah.

13 His offering was one silver plate weighing a hundred and thirty shekels, and one silver sprinkling bowl weighing seventy shekels, both according to the sanctuary shekel, each filled with fine flour mixed with oil as a grain offering; 14 one gold dish weighing ten shekels, filled with incense; 15 one young bull, one ram and one male lamb a year old, for a burnt offering; 16 one male goat for a sin offering; 17 and two oxen, five rams, five male goats and five male lambs a year old, to be sacrificed as a fellowship offering. This was the offering of Nahshon son of Amminadab.

18 On the second day Nethanel son of Zuar, the leader of Issachar, brought his offering.

19 The offering he brought was one silver plate weighing a hundred and thirty shekels, and one silver sprinkling bowl

weighing seventy shekels, both according to the sanctuary shekel, each filled with fine flour mixed with oil as a grain offering; ²⁰one gold dish weighing ten shekels, filled with incense; ²¹one young bull, one ram and one male lamb a year old, for a burnt offering; ²²one male goat for a sin offering; ²³and two oxen, five rams, five male goats and five male lambs a year old, to be sacrificed as a fellowship offering. This was the offering of Nethanel son of Zuar.

²⁴On the third day Eliab son of Helon, the leader of the people of Zebulun, brought his offering.

²⁵His offering was one silver plate weighing a hundred and thirty shekels, and one silver sprinkling bowl weighing seventy shekels, both according to the sanctuary shekel, each filled with fine flour mixed with oil as a grain offering; ²⁶one gold dish weighing ten shekels, filled with incense; ²⁷one young bull, one ram and one male lamb a year old, for a burnt offering; ²⁸one male goat for a sin offering; ²⁹and two oxen, five rams, five male goats and five male lambs a year old, to be sacrificed as a fellowship offering. This was the offering of Eliab son of Helon.

³⁰On the fourth day Elizur son of Shedeur, the leader of the people of Reuben, brought his offering.

³¹His offering was one silver plate weighing a hundred and thirty shekels, and one silver sprinkling bowl weighing seventy shekels, both according to the sanctuary shekel, each filled with fine flour mixed with oil as a grain offering; ³²one gold dish weighing ten shekels, filled with incense; ³³one young bull, one ram and one male lamb a year old, for a burnt offering; ³⁴one male goat for a sin offering; ³⁵and two oxen, five rams, five male goats and five male lambs a year old, to be sacrificed as a fellowship offering. This was the offering of Elizur son of Shedeur.

³⁶On the fifth day Shelumiel son of Zurishaddai, the leader of the people of Simeon, brought his offering.

³⁷His offering was one silver plate weighing a hundred and thirty shekels, and one silver sprinkling bowl weighing

seventy shekels, both according to the sanctuary shekel, each filled with fine flour mixed with oil as a grain offering; [38]one gold dish weighing ten shekels, filled with incense; [39]one young bull, one ram and one male lamb a year old, for a burnt offering; [40]one male goat for a sin offering; [41]and two oxen, five rams, five male goats and five male lambs a year old, to be sacrificed as a fellowship offering. This was the offering of Shelumiel son of Zurishaddai.

[42]On the sixth day Eliasaph son of Deuel, the leader of the people of Gad, brought his offering.

[43]His offering was one silver plate weighing a hundred and thirty shekels, and one silver sprinkling bowl weighing seventy shekels, both according to the sanctuary shekel, each filled with fine flour mixed with oil as a grain offering; [44]one gold dish weighing ten shekels, filled with incense; [45]one young bull, one ram and one male lamb a year old, for a burnt offering; [46]one male goat for a sin offering; [47]and two oxen, five rams, five male goats and five male lambs a year old, to be sacrificed as a fellowship offering. This was the offering of Eliasaph son of Deuel.

[48]On the seventh day Elishama son of Ammihud, the leader of the people of Ephraim, brought his offering.

[49]His offering was one silver plate weighing a hundred and thirty shekels, and one silver sprinkling bowl weighing seventy shekels, both according to the sanctuary shekel, each filled with fine flour mixed with oil as a grain offering; [50]one gold dish weighing ten shekels, filled with incense; [51]one young bull, one ram and one male lamb a year old, for a burnt offering; [52]one male goat for a sin offering; [53]and two oxen, five rams, five male goats and five male lambs a year old, to be sacrificed as a fellowship offering. This was the offering of Elishama son of Ammihud.

[54]On the eighth day Gamaliel son of Pedahzur, the leader of the people of Manasseh, brought his offering.

[55]His offering was one silver plate weighing a hundred and thirty shekels, and one silver sprinkling bowl weighing

seventy shekels, both according to the sanctuary shekel, each filled with fine flour mixed with oil as a grain offering; [56]one gold dish weighing ten shekels, filled with incense; [57]one young bull, one ram and one male lamb a year old, for a burnt offering; [58]one male goat for a sin offering; [59]and two oxen, five rams, five male goats and five male lambs a year old, to be sacrificed as a fellowship offering. This was the offering of Gamaliel son of Pedahzur.

[60]On the ninth day Abidan son of Gideoni, the leader of the people of Benjamin, brought his offering.

[61]His offering was one silver plate weighing a hundred and thirty shekels, and one silver sprinkling bowl weighing seventy shekels, both according to the sanctuary shekel, each filled with fine flour mixed with oil as a grain offering; [62]one gold dish weighing ten shekels, filled with incense; [63]one young bull, one ram and one male lamb a year old, for a burnt offering; [64]one male goat for a sin offering; [65]and two oxen, five rams, five male goats and five male lambs a year old, to be sacrificed as a fellowship offering. This was the offering of Abidan son of Gideoni.

[66]On the tenth day Ahiezer son of Ammishaddai, the leader of the people of Dan, brought his offering.

[67]His offering was one silver plate weighing a hundred and thirty shekels, and one silver sprinkling bowl weighing seventy shekels, both according to the sanctuary shekel, each filled with fine flour mixed with oil as a grain offering; [68]one gold dish weighing ten shekels, filled with incense; [69]one young bull, one ram and one male lamb a year old, for a burnt offering; [70]one male goat for a sin offering; [71]and two oxen, five rams, five male goats and five male lambs a year old, to be sacrificed as a fellowship offering. This was the offering of Ahiezer son of Ammishaddai.

[72]On the eleventh day Pagiel son of Ocran, the leader of the people of Asher, brought his offering.

[73]His offering was one silver plate weighing a hundred and thirty shekels, and one silver sprinkling bowl weighing

seventy shekels, both according to the sanctuary shekel, each filled with fine flour mixed with oil as a grain offering; [74]one gold dish weighing ten shekels, filled with incense; [75]one young bull, one ram and one male lamb a year old, for a burnt offering; [76]one male goat for a sin offering; [77]and two oxen, five rams, five male goats and five male lambs a year old, to be sacrificed as a fellowship offering. This was the offering of Pagiel son of Ocran.

[78]On the twelfth day Ahira son of Enan, the leader of the people of Naphtali, brought his offering.

[79]His offering was one silver plate weighing a hundred and thirty shekels, and one silver sprinkling bowl weighing seventy shekels, both according to the sanctuary shekel, each filled with fine flour mixed with oil as a grain offering; [80]one gold dish weighing ten shekels, filled with incense; [81]one young bull, one ram and one male lamb a year old, for a burnt offering; [82]one male goat for a sin offering; [83]and two oxen, five rams, five male goats and five male lambs a year old, to be sacrificed as a fellowship offering. This was the offering of Ahira son of Enan.

[84]These were the offerings of the Israelite leaders for the dedication of the altar when it was anointed: twelve silver plates, twelve silver sprinkling bowls and twelve gold dishes. [85]Each silver plate weighed a hundred and thirty shekels, and each sprinkling bowl seventy shekels. Altogether, the silver dishes weighed two thousand four hundred shekels, according to the sanctuary shekel. [86]The twelve gold dishes filled with incense weighed ten shekels each, according to the sanctuary shekel. Altogether, the gold dishes weighed a hundred and twenty shekels. [87]The total number of animals for the burnt offering came to twelve young bulls, twelve rams and twelve male lambs a year old, together with their grain offering. Twelve male goats were used for the sin offering. [88]The total number of animals for the sacrifice of the fellowship offering came to twenty-four oxen, sixty rams, sixty male goats and sixty male lambs a year old. These were the offerings for the dedication of the altar after it was anointed.

Generous offerings were presented at the time of the dedication of the altar by the princes on behalf of each tribe of Israel. In recording these events the Holy Spirit very carefully lists each gift separately to show that the Lord knows, acknowledges and takes pleasure in the gifts of each individual. A person is certainly also reminded of our Savior's acknowledgement and comments about the individual gift a poor widow brought to the temple (Luke 21:1ff).

In reviewing these gifts it is interesting to note that the gifts are identical, although there was a considerable difference in the size of the twelve tribes. Clearly this was to show that each tribe was equally a part of the chosen nation, was equally in need of God's covenant of grace and would share equally in the covenant blessings.

The gift of each tribe can be divided into three categories: three items became part of the equipment for the tabernacle (a silver dish, a silver bowl, a gold pan full of incense); three animals were consumed in sacrifices (a bull, a ram for a burnt offering and a goat for a sin offering) and the fellowship offerings consisting of seventeen animals (two oxen, five rams, five goats and five year-old lambs). Since the fellowship offerings ended in a festive meal that celebrated fellowship with God, it is assumed that in some way representatives of each tribe participated in the festive meal of the fellowship offerings. Like the dinners that are served at church dedications in our day, the festive meal of the peace offering provided a way in which members of each tribe were able to enjoy the fact that the covenant relationship with God was real. This was especially true in connection with the dedication of the altar. The message of the sacrifices presented the positive note that the Lord graciously chose to reaffirm their covenant relationship through the sin offering and the burnt offering. This significance was true even as the sin offering and burnt offering really had their value before God only because they pointed forward to the sacrifice of Christ on the cross.

The Lord Speaks to Moses from the Most Holy Place

89 When Moses entered the Tent of Meeting to speak with the LORD, he heard the voice speaking to him from between the two cherubim above the atonement cover on the ark of the Testimony. And he spoke with him.

This verse gives us information about the method that the Lord used in speaking with Moses. The Lord did manifest his glory at the Tent of Meeting at the conclusion of the gifts offered by the twelve leaders of Israel.

Earlier, when God was consecrating the priesthood by his presence, he used a full manifestation of his glory in the sight of all (Leviticus 9). By this action God showed that in the Old Testament covenant he would be dealing with the people through a priesthood. As the Lord now wished to acknowledge the gifts of the tribal leaders, he chose to use the form of his presence that would be ongoing in the tabernacle. Therefore as the twelve days of offering were completed, Moses went into the Tent of Meeting and the Lord spoke to him from the space above the ark of the Testimony and between the two golden cherubim. This manifestation of God's presence had already been promised to Moses when he received instructions about building the tabernacle (Exodus 25:22). The fulfillment of the promise had been reported in Leviticus 16:2 in connection with the instructions for the Great Day of Atonement

As the Lord manifested his continuing presence in the Most Holy Place, it is clear that he was pleased that the children of Israel had been carefully obedient in preparing and equipping the tabernacle. Though the Lord cannot be contained in temples made with human hands, it certainly was a high privilege that the children of Israel enjoyed! The Lord God chose to manifest himself in their tabernacle! He spoke to Moses directly from the space above the Ark of Testimony in the Most Holy Place. Truly such a manifestation of the Lord's presence, coming as it did after the gifts of the princes, showed that the Lord was pleased to accept the entire nation as the people of the covenant.

The Hebrew verb forms in this verse express continued activity. Therefore the statement here is best understood to mean that from this point onward Moses received divine messages in the Most Holy Place at the mercy seat. The solemn words: "The LORD spoke to Moses" indicate that Moses was present in the tabernacle and the Lord then spoke to him from the Most Holy Place.

Setting Up the Lamps

8 **The LORD said to Moses, ²"Speak to Aaron and say to him, 'When you set up the seven lamps, they are to light the area in front of the lampstand.' "**

³Aaron did so; he set up the lamps so that they faced forward on the lampstand, just as the LORD commanded Moses. ⁴This is how the lampstand was made: It was made of hammered gold — from its base to its blossoms. The lampstand was made exactly like the pattern the LORD had shown Moses.

The lampstands referred to here are described in greater detail in Exodus 25:31-40. They were made of hammered gold. Once again bringing such rich gifts for the service of the Lord is an example for believers of all ages. Truly we feel an inner compulsion to offer the Lord the very best gifts we can in our places of worship.

The instructions here focus on the position of the lampstands in the tabernacle. It was necessary to have such lamps inside the tabernacle because there were no windows. The lamps on the lampstands were to be positioned so that the light would fall in front of the lampstand. As these lamps stood before the Most Holy Place they symbolized the idea that all true light comes from the Lord.

Instructions for Setting the Levites Apart

⁵The LORD said to Moses: ⁶"Take the Levites from among the other Israelites and make them ceremonially clean. ⁷To purify them, do this: Sprinkle the water of cleansing on them; then have them shave their whole bodies and wash their clothes, and so purify themselves. ⁸Have them take a young bull with its grain offering of fine flour mixed with oil; then you are to take a second young bull for a sin offering. ⁹Bring the Levites to the front of the Tent of Meeting and assemble the whole Israelite community. ¹⁰You are to bring the Levites before the LORD, and the Israelites are to lay their hands on them. ¹¹Aaron is to present the Levites before the LORD as a wave offering from the Israelites, so that they may be ready to do the work of the LORD.

¹²"After the Levites lay their hands on the heads of he bulls, use the one for a sin offering to the LORD and the other for a burnt offering, to make atonement for the Levites. ¹³Have the Levites stand in front of Aaron and his sons and then present them as a wave offering to the LORD. ¹⁴In this way you are to set the Levites apart from the other Israelites, and the Levites will be mine.

¹⁵"After you have purified the Levites and presented them as a wave offering, they are to come to do their work at the Tent of Meeting. ¹⁶They are the Israelites who are to be given wholly to me. I have taken them as my own in place of the firstborn, the first male offspring from every Israelite woman. ¹⁷Every firstborn male in Israel, whether man or animal, is mine. When I struck down all the firstborn in Egypt, I set them apart for myself. ¹⁸And I have taken the Levites in place of all the firstborn sons in Israel. ¹⁹Of all the Israelites, I have given the Levites as gifts to Aaron and his sons to do the work at the Tent of Meeting on behalf of the

Israelites and to make atonement for them so that no plague will strike the Israelites when they go near the sanctuary."

Through the ritual that the Lord here prescribes, the Levites were to be inducted into their responsibilities at the tabernacle.

The first step of the ritual was to make the Levites ceremonially clean. They were to be sprinkled with the water of cleansing. Thereupon they were to shave their whole bodies and wash their clothes. The second step was that a burnt offering and a sin offering were to be made on their behalf. For the Levites there was also the truth that they could not dedicate themselves to the Lord for service in his house without first offering a sacrifice for their own sins.

In a solemn assembly of the community of Israel, the fact that the Levites were substituting for the people, especially the firstborn, was to be demonstrated by the laying on of hands. Then the Levites were to be presented as a wave offering before the Lord. In the wave offering the sacrifice (here the Levites) was not consumed in the fire but was merely moved to and fro before the Lord and was thus presented for use in his service.

This whole ritual was based on the fact that at Mount Sinai the Lord had claimed the Levites as his own in place of all the firstborn males in Israel. The Lord's claim to the firstborn on the basis of the Passover in Egypt is explained again.

Through this ritual the Levites were to be presented to Aaron and the priests to do the work at the Tent of Meeting. In a carefully structured order of responsibility, the priests were to make the actual sacrifices and function in the Holy Place. The Levites were to help the priests as assistants and were to do the many tasks involved in maintaining the tabernacle. The people, however, were not allowed to enter the Tent of Meeting. The Lord had determined that the people were to approach him only through the appointed priests and Levites.

Consecration of the Levites and Their Length of Service

20 Moses, Aaron and the whole Israelite community did with the Levites just as the LORD commanded Moses. 21 The Levites purified themselves and washed their clothes. Then Aaron presented them as a wave offering before the LORD and made atonement for them to purify them. 22 After that, the Levites came to do their work at the Tent of Meeting under the supervision of Aaron and his sons. They did with the Levites just as the LORD commanded Moses.

23 The LORD said to Moses, 24 "This applies to the Levites: Men twenty-five years old or more shall come to take part in the work at the Tent of Meeting, 25 but at the age of fifty, they must retire from their regular service and work no longer. 26 They may assist their brothers in performing their duties at the Tent of Meeting, but they themselves must not do the work. This, then, is how you are to assign the responsibilities of the Levites."

Again it is noted how faithfully the people followed the commands of the Lord. The Levites were consecrated for their duties according to a solemn ritual. Thereupon they immediately began to function at the Tent of Meeting.

Then the Lord defined the age limits that were to apply to the service of the Levites. They were to serve actively at the Tent of Meeting from the age of twenty-five to the age of fifty. Apparently from age twenty-five to thirty the Levites would be apprenticed as helpers (see Numbers 4:3,4, where the age of thirty is mentioned) — that is, they would be learning what their tasks were. After the age of fifty Levites would also be allowed to assist, but would not be allowed actually to do the work of the Tent of Meeting.

Once again we note how carefully the Lord defines and assigns responsibilities. There was to be no excuse. Every reasonable effort was made to prevent the service in the tabernacle from being defiled through ignorance or carelessness. If there was ignorance or carelessness, the guilt would lie entirely on the individual who ignored the Lord's instructions.

Throughout these early sections the fact that our Lord is a God of order comes through again and again. The church through all ages would do well to take careful note of this fact.

Celebration of the Passover

9 **The LORD spoke to Moses in the Desert of Sinai in the first month of the second year after they came out of Egypt. He said, ²"Have the Israelites celebrate the Passover at the appointed time. ³Celebrate it at the appointed time, at twilight on the fourteenth day of this month, in accordance with all its rules and regulations."**

⁴So Moses told the Israelites to celebrate the Passover, ⁵and they did so in the Desert of Sinai at twilight on the fourteenth day of the first month. The Israelites did everything just as the LORD commanded Moses.

One year had passed since the mighty hand of the Lord had rescued the Israelites from Egypt. God had ordained that the people were to observe the Passover to commemorate the night of deliverance. In solemn remembrance the Israelites were to celebrate the fact that the angel of the Lord had passed over their homes, but had entered every Egyptian house and killed the firstborn.

A busy year had passed. Many very dramatic moments had occurred. The delivery from Egypt, the escape through the Red Sea, the awesome appearance of the Lord on

Mount Sinai, the busy days and months of preparing the Tent of Meeting with all its equipment, the joyous days of the month-long celebration of dedication—all of these events had taken place. How wondrously the Lord had kept his promise to deliver the Israelites and to establish them as his covenant people through whom the promised Messiah would come.

As a year had passed it was time again to celebrate the Passover with all its rules and regulations. On the fourteenth day of the first month the children of Israel celebrated their first commemorative Passover. Such celebrations were repeated each year until the coming of Christ. At that point the predictive and symbolical elements of the Passover were fulfilled. The slaughtered lamb and the blood on the doorposts reached their fulfillment in the Lamb of God, whose blood cleanses us from all sin.

"Why Should We Be Kept from Celebrating the Passover?"

6But some of them could not celebrate the Passover on that day because they were ceremonially unclean on account of a dead body. So they came to Moses and Aaron that same day 7and said to Moses, "We have become unclean because of a dead body, but why should we be kept from presenting the LORD's offering with the other Israelites at the appointed time?"

8Moses answered them, "Wait until I find out what the LORD commands concerning you."

9Then the LORD said to Moses, 10"Tell the Israelites: 'When any of you or your descendants are unclean because of a dead body or are away on a journey, they may still celebrate the LORD's Passover. 11They are to celebrate it on the fourteenth day of the second month at twilight. They are to eat the lamb, together with unleavened bread and bitter herbs. 12They must not leave any of it till morning or break any of its bones. When they celebrate the Passover, they must follow all the regulations. 13But if a man who

is ceremonially clean and not on a journey fails to celebrate the Passover, that person must be cut off from his people because he did not present the LORD's offering at the appointed time. That man will bear the consequences of his sin.

14" 'An alien living among you who wants to celebrate the LORD's Passover must do so in accordance with its rules and regulations. You must have the same regulations for the alien and the native-born.' "

Some people had been in contact with a dead body and were therefore ceremonially unclean on the fourteenth day of the first month. As a result they were excluded from celebrating the Passover. Yet their desire to worship the Lord on this festal occasion shows through very clearly in their question, "Why should we be kept from presenting the LORD's offering?"

As a true servant of God, Moses did not answer impulsively. Since he had no previous instruction, he asked them to wait until he had a chance to get an answer from the Lord.

The Lord's answer allowed for two exceptional situations — when a person had become unclean because of a dead body and when a person was away on a journey. In these two exceptional situations the people were allowed to celebrate the Passover exactly one month later. Even though the alternate time became known as the "Little Passover," it was to be the only exception. All other rules and regulations were to be followed in their entirety.

Yet the Lord shows clearly that he knows the nature of sinful human beings. First, there were to be no shortcuts in the celebration by those who celebrated the Passover a month later. Just as surely the establishment of the "Little Passover" was not an easy excuse for those who might find it inconvenient to celebrate on the appointed day. Indeed, those who did not meet the two criteria for delaying the

Passover and still failed to celebrate the Passover at the designated time were to be cut off from the people, that is, they were to be excommunicated.

One other instruction needed expression: The same rules and regulations for the Passover applied both to the native-born of the Israelites as well as to any alien who chose to join in the celebration of the Passover.

FROM SINAI TO KADESH

Life While Moving Out

The fourth general topic of the first section of Numbers focuses on the trek from Sinai to Kadesh. After more than a full year the Lord was ready to lead his chosen people to the promised land. To lead them he provided a pillar of cloud and a pillar of fire. To keep them in order he directed that silver trumpets be used like bugles.

So the trek began. But with the travel came a growing rebelliousness against the Lord. There were some general complaints among the hangers-on that had come along from Egypt. Then came the complaints about food. Even Aaron and Miriam turned on Moses. Finally the people followed the majority report of the spies who had gone to Canaan and refused to go forward under the blessing of the Lord.

In this series of events the patience of the Lord was sorely tried and he determined that not one person from the people who were twenty years old and older when they left Egypt would enter the Promised Land. As God's chastisement, the people were compelled to wander for forty years in the wilderness.

The Cloud Above the Tabernacle

15On the day the tabernacle, the Tent of the Testimony, was set up, the cloud covered it. From evening till morning the cloud above the tabernacle looked like fire. 16That is how it continued to be; the cloud covered it, and at night it looked like fire. 17Whenever the cloud lifted from above the Tent, the Israelites set out;

**wherever the cloud settled, the Israelites encamped. [18]At the
LORD's command the Israelites set out, and at his command they
encamped. As long as the cloud stayed over the tabernacle, they
remained in camp. [19]When the cloud remained over the tabernacle a long time, the Israelites obeyed the LORD's order and did
not set out. [20]Sometimes the cloud was over the tabernacle only a
few days; at the LORD's command they would encamp, and then at
his command they would set out. [21]Sometimes the cloud stayed
only from evening till morning, and when it lifted in the morning,
they set out. Whether by day or by night, whenever the cloud
lifted, they set out. [22]Whether the cloud stayed over the tabernacle
for two days or a month or a year, the Israelites would remain in
camp and not set out; but when it lifted, they would set out. [23]At
the LORD's command they encamped, and at the LORD's command they set out. They obeyed the LORD's order, in accordance
with his command through Moses.**

The previous section looked backward to the deliverance
from Egypt. For approximately a year the children of Israel
had encamped at Mount Sinai. The events that occurred
during the encampment are recorded in the account from
Exodus 19 to the first part of the present chapter. The
present section serves as a transition and looks forward to
the journey to the Promised Land. In overview Moses sum-
marized the procedure by which the Lord gave the Israelites
their marching orders. Through the remaining years of desert wandering, the Lord used the cloud that hovered over
the tabernacle to give the signals.

The cloud of the Lord had first appeared to cut off the
Egyptian army at the Red Sea. It then guided the entire
nation to the foot of Mount Sinai.

The pillar of cloud/fire took a prominent place in the
dedication of the tabernacle (Exodus 40). The cloud entered
and filled the entire Tent of Meeting. The Lord, who indicated his presence as a God of grace by his presence

between the cherubim in the Most Holy Place, also indicated his presence as the leader and protector of Israel by the cloud/fire that hovered over the tabernacle. Continuously, at any time of day or night, an Israelite was able to look toward the tabernacle and remind himself that even in the hostile environment of the desert the Lord was the leader and protector of the people he had chosen as his own.

The signals, which the Lord used to guide the nation, were simple and direct. When the cloud lifted, the children of Israel would move out from their camp. Then wherever the cloud settled down the children of Israel would encamp. The position of the cloud was "in the sight" (Exodus 40:38) of the whole camp. So by an unmistakable visual signal the whole mass of people could be controlled.

From Sinai to the entrance to the Promised Land the cloud of the Lord's presence continued to be with the Israelites. This point is the main emphasis of the statement in Exodus 40:36-38, where Moses twice used the phrase "throughout all their journeys."

The emphasis in the present section is somewhat different. Since the position of the cloud indicated the Lord's will, the children of Israel could tell at a glance what the "orders of the day" were. Eight times in this eight verse paragraph there is a direct statement that the position of the cloud was a command or charge from the Lord. How clearly this shows that the entire journey through the wilderness was directed by God! The only mention of Moses, the human leader, is in the last phrase and even then his function is clearly dependent on the word of the Lord — "in accordance with his [God's] command through Moses." Everything, whether it was the daily supply of manna, or providing water at Marah, or the decision to move the camp — everything depended on the Lord's will.

On the other hand, the biblical record also shows that the children of Israel did obey their marching orders faithfully. There were all too many other situations in which the people disobeyed the Lord. Yet just as the Scriptures report sin, they also give credit where credit is due. It was commendable that the Israelites faithfully kept the charge of the Lord in moving the camp. With this thought in mind the many references to time in this paragraph do not seem unduly repetitious.

Their obedience to the "order of the day" was evident in those periods when the cloud remained stationary over the tabernacle for "many days." Even though the cycle of days in the desert became tedious and wearisome, the Israelites remained in their camp. On the other hand, even if they had had time to make their nomadic life more comfortable during a stay of many days, whenever the cloud did lift, they would obediently break camp. The same submission to the Lord's will was evident if the encampment was for only a "few days." Even though they might be impatient to move on, the Israelites would stay in camp until the Lord gave the word. Then as soon as the cloud lifted, even though they didn't know which day it might be, they would take down their tents, load up their belongings and move on. Nor were they less obedient if the cloud stayed over the tabernacle only "from evening to morning." Then even though their feet were sore from walking and their backs aching from carrying their possessions, they would set out again. In these ways the Israelites looked to the Lord for daily guidance. Before they could make their plans for the day, they would have to check on the position of the cloud. Should the day be one in which the cloud was lifted up, the people would lay their plans aside and move out. Each day was controlled by the Lord, and they obeyed the Lord's command, whether it meant they stayed in camp for "two days or a month or a year."

It is a joy to reflect on this positive aspect of the obedience of the children of Israel. In the chapters still to come there will be opportunity enough to point to warning examples when they did not obey.

The cloud served to emphasize the dependence of the Israelites on the Lord. It also showed his providential care for them. In fact whenever we place our plans for daily life under the gracious direction of the Lord, we will find that the Lord's ways are always good. Such obedience and confidence in the Lord's guidance is also included when we pray, "Thy will be done on earth as it is in heaven. Give us this day our daily bread."

The Silver Trumpets

10 The LORD said to Moses: ²"Make two trumpets of hammered silver, and use them for calling the community together and for having the camps set out. ³When both are sounded, the whole community is to assemble before you at the entrance to the Tent of Meeting. ⁴If only one is sounded, the leaders — the heads of the clans of Israel — are to assemble before you. ⁵When a trumpet blast is sounded, the tribes camping on the east are to set out. ⁶At the sounding of a second blast, the camps on the south are to set out. The blast will be the signal for setting out. ⁷To gather the assembly, blow the trumpets, but not with the same signal.

⁸"The sons of Aaron, the priests, are to blow the trumpets. This is to be a lasting ordinance for you and the generations to come. ⁹When you go into battle in your own land against an enemy who is oppressing you, sound a blast on the trumpets. Then you will be remembered by the LORD your God and rescued from your enemies. ¹⁰Also at your times of rejoicing — your appointed feasts and New Moon festivals — you are to sound the trumpets over

your burnt offerings and fellowship offerings, and they will be a memorial for you before your God. I am the LORD your God."

It has been mentioned on several occasions that the Lord gave a number of instructions designed to provide good order for the Israelites. The information about the silver trumpets serves the same purpose.

Two trumpets of hammered silver were to be made. They served in the same way a bugle served for cavalry troops in more recent times. The trumpets had three functions during the times the Israelites were in the wilderness. The first was to summon the entire community of Israel for a solemn assembly. Two trumpets would be blown to announce such a meeting. The second function was to summon the clan leaders for a meeting. One trumpet would be blown for such a meeting. The third function was to give signals for an orderly departure from an encampment. A trumpet blast would sound when each of the four divisions of the camp was to set out. Though the lifting of the cloud from the tabernacle would indicate that it was the day to set out, the blasts on the trumpets would signal the exact time for each of the divisions to set out. In this way the camp was able to continue its journey in an orderly fashion.

The Lord also defined two future uses of the trumpets. Though the nation was not yet in its land of promise, the Lord's prophecies made it sure. So when they would be in the Promised Land, if they felt that they had to go to war against an enemy, they were to sound the trumpets. In such a case the Lord promised that "then you will be remembered by the Lord your God and rescued from your enemies." The second future use was a joyous sounding of the trumpets when the children of Israel were celebrating their appointed festivals. On such occasions the trumpets would call the people to worship and lead them in it.

As a lasting ordinance the arrangement was made that the priests were the ones who were to sound the trumpets. This may seem a bit strange at first since several of the uses had nothing to do with priestly functions. Yet when we realize that the Lord was establishing a theocracy in which he as God was the commander-in-chief, this arrangement seems most natural. The Lord was dwelling in the tabernacle. At the tabernacle he would make his will known. The priests who functioned at the tabernacle would be among the first to know the will of the Lord. Therefore they were the logical ones to sound the trumpets in order to spread the message.

In general, whether in war or on festive occasions, the blast of the silver trumpet had the spiritual meaning: "They will be a memorial for you before your God." In other words, Israel was a host and as such could be summoned by the blast of a trumpet. But Israel was a host of which Jehovah was leader and king, and the trumpets that summoned this host were the silver trumpets of the sanctuary, blown by the priests of the Lord. Such trumpet blasts brought Israel together as the Lord's host before their God and king.

When Moses reported that the "manufacturing" of the trumpets was finished, everything the Lord had commanded was complete. Now the nation was ready to depart from the wilderness of Sinai.

The Israelites Leave Sinai

[11]On the twentieth day of the second month of the second year, the cloud lifted from above the tabernacle of the Testimony. [12]Then the Israelites set out from the Desert of Sinai and traveled from place to place until the cloud came to rest in the Desert of Paran. [13]They set out, this first time, at the LORD's command through Moses.

¹⁴The divisions of the camp of Judah went first, under their standard. Nahshon son of Amminadab was in command. ¹⁵Nethanel son of Zuar was over the division of the tribe of Issachar, ¹⁶and Eliab son of Helon was over the division of the tribe of Zebulun. ¹⁷ Then the tabernacle was taken down, and the Gershonites and Merarites, who carried it, set out.

¹⁸The divisions of the camp of Reuben went next, under their standard. Elizur son of Shedeur was in command. ¹⁹Shelumiel son of Zurishaddai was over the division of the tribe of Simeon, ²⁰and Eliasaph son of Deuel was over the division of the tribe of Gad. ²¹Then the Kohathites set out, carrying the holy things. The tabernacle was to be set up before they arrived.

²²The divisions of the camp of Ephraim went next, under their standard. Elishama son of Ammihud was in command. ²³Gamaliel son of Pedahzur was over the division of the tribe of Manasseh, ²⁴and Abidan son of Gideoni was over the division of the tribe of Benjamin.

²⁵Finally, as the rear guard for all the units, the divisions of the camp of Dan set out, under their standard. Ahiezer son of Ammishaddai was in command. ²⁶Pagiel son of Ocran was over the division of the tribe of Asher, ²⁷and Ahira son of Enan was over the division of the tribe of Naphtali. ²⁸This was the order of march for the Israelite divisions as they set out.

The Lord had delivered Israel from Egypt and led them to Sinai. During their year-long encampment at Sinai God had established his covenant with the Israelites and reestablished it again after the idolatry of the golden calf. The tabernacle and its furnishings had been made and dedicated. The priests and Levites had been installed into their respective offices. The people had been counted and organized for the camp and for the march. So the natural next step was that the cloud be lifted from the tabernacle and that the Lord would lead the Israelites to the Promised Land. The departure from Sinai took place in the second year, the second month, the twentieth day of the month after the deliverance from Egypt. The departure was timed to allow an opportunity for those Israelites to celebrate the Passover who because of ceremonial uncleanness hadn't been able to celebrate the festival at its regular time a month earlier (see Numbers 9:10f).

Moses again points out the faithfulness of the children of Israel in following the marching orders of the Lord. The people moved into the line of march in exactly the order that the Lord had prescribed. When the order of march is listed in this way it is easy to see the practical wisdom in the arrangement of the Levites, who were to carry the tabernacle.

The Gershonites and Merarites set out early, because they transported the framework and the coverings for the tabernacle. At the end of the day's march they would be able to set up the entire tabernacle before the Kohathites arrived. The Kohathites were then able to put all the holy things in place and the tabernacle would be completely in service by the time the rest of the children of Israel had finished setting up camp.

Moses Invites Hobab to Join Israel

29Now Moses said to Hobab son of Reuel the Midianite, Moses' father-in-law, "We are setting out for the place about which the LORD said, 'I will give it to you.' Come with us and we will treat you well, for the LORD has promised good things to Israel."

30He answered, "No, I will not go; I am going back to my own land and my own people."

31But Moses said "Please do not leave us. You know where we should camp in the desert, and you can be our eyes. 32If you come with us, we will share with you whatever good things the LORD gives us."

While the Israelites were staying at Sinai they were in the region where the family of Moses' wife lived. At the time of departure Moses invited his brother-in-law Hobab to accompany them. Moses pointed to the blessings Hobab would receive. He would certainly be blessed by the fact that the people would treat him well. But even more, Hobab would be blessed by the fact that the Lord had "promised good things to Israel." Moses knew that the grace and love in the formula, "I will be your God and you shall be my people" is extended also to anyone who casts his lot with God's people.

Though Hobab declined the invitation, Moses persisted. He added the fact that Hobab's knowledge of the desert area would serve Israel well. It is a bit jarring to note that Moses suggested that Hobab could help in picking campsites. This seems to contradict the fact that the Lord was going to pick the camping area through the pillar of cloud. It is unacceptable to say that Moses would contradict the Lord. The answer probably lies in the second part where Moses indicates that Hobab could be "eyes" for the children of Israel. Such eyes could indeed provide a great service. The eyes of an experienced desert dweller could pick up clues about the presence of water, either in oases or in sheltered areas where water from the rare rains gathers, that the inexperienced eye would never see.

The report at this point does not indicate whether Hobab went with Israel or not. Later in Judges 1:16 arrangements are made so that the descendants of Hobab would receive a portion of the Promised Land with the tribe of Judah. So Hobab apparently did cast his lot with the Israelites.

Three Days' Journey and a Ritual Established

33So they set out from the mountain of the LORD and traveled for three days. The ark of the covenant of the LORD went before

90

them during those three days to find them a place to rest. ³⁴The cloud of the LORD was over them by day when they set out from the camp.

³⁵Whenever the ark set out, Moses said,

> "Rise up, O LORD!
>> May your enemies be scattered;
>> may your foes flee before you."

³⁶Whenever it came to rest, he said,

> "Return, O LORD,
>> to the countless thousands of Israel."

Three days in a row the Lord lifted his cloud from the tabernacle as the children of Israel marched through the desert of Sinai. At this point the information is given that the ark of the covenant was carried at the front of the column when they traveled. Apparently the ark was taken immediately from the Tent of Meeting as the march began and was placed at the very head of the marching column. Obviously it was the cloud of the Lord that was over the ark that really was leading the Israelites.

During those three days Moses also established a ritual that he followed whenever the ark set out. The words that he spoke focused on the cloud as the solemn assurance that the Lord was present with his people. When the ark would set out Moses would proclaim, "Rise up, O LORD! May your enemies be scattered; may your foes flee before you." The Lord was leading the people! The Lord had given the people their marching orders! The Lord would be the One who scattered the enemies before Israel. The Lord was vitally involved since everyone who opposed Israel was really opposing him. The Lord would be victorious even over those that hated him. Such was the confidence that Israel could have as they followed the manifestation of God's presence in the pillar of cloud/fire through the wilderness.

When the ark came to rest at the place where the cloud had settled to the ground, Moses would say, "Return, O Lord, to the countless thousands of Israel." God is here presented as a conquering hero who is returning to his people. So Moses prayed that the Lord would again turn his attention to the daily care of the thousands of Israel. Each day the Israelites had reason to praise and glorify the Lord, who had scattered and put the enemies to flight.

Moses expressed the bold confidence of faith. Here is a prayer which will surely be heard. Oh, that Christians in every age would pray with such confidence! The whole church of Christ has indeed overcome the forces of darkness in the strength of the Lord. Moses also had the confidence that the gates of hell cannot prevail against the Lord. Every Christian knows that it is God who keeps him in all his ways, who defends him from all harm and danger even in the night season. In such confidence we pray "Deliver us from evil."

Fire from the Lord

11 **Now the people complained about their hardships in the hearing of the Lord, and when he heard them his anger was aroused. Then the fire from the Lord burned among them and consumed some of the outskirts of the camp. ²When the people cried out to Moses, he prayed to the Lord and the fire died down. ³So that place was called Taberah, because fire from the Lord had burned among them.**

This paragraph is the beginning of a series of incidents which show how the attitude of the Israelites degenerated from some general griping to open rebellion against the Lord. How bold the contrast with the many times that they showed the strict and faithful obedience they had promised at the encampment at Mount Sinai! How jarring it is to note that the mood of the people changes so completely. It changes from obeying the Lord in every detail to thankless complaining against the Lord.

Only three days of travel and the people were already complaining about the hardships. The Bible does not clearly define the complaints. The generalized griping very likely blamed God for sore feet, sore backs and sore muscles.

The Lord was provoked by their attitude! He recognized the seriousness and sought to cut off the sin in its first beginning. Therefore fire from the Lord burned among them and consumed some of the outskirts of the camp. Apparently no human beings were destroyed and yet their fear must have been like the fear people have of a prairie fire raging out of control. Although there is no indication of the origin of the fire, by calling it "fire from the LORD" the Bible makes it clear that the Lord was directing events whether he used natural means or miraculous means.

Jarred to their senses, the people appealed to Moses. He was a proven mediator with God. In answer to Moses' prayer the Lord quenched the fire.

The event caused the children of Israel to name the place Taberah, which means "burning."

When God's children murmur against his fatherly treatment he finds it necessary occasionally to discipline them. But when they cry out to him with repentant hearts, he turns again with the fullness of his grace and mercy. In the case of the children of Israel, however, the merciful warning went essentially unheeded. The complaints only accelerated.

The Desire for Meat Puts Moses in the Middle

⁴The rabble with them began to crave other food, and again the Israelites started wailing and said, "If only we had meat to eat! ⁵We remember the fish we ate in Egypt at no cost — also the cucumbers, melons, leeks, onions and garlic. ⁶But now we have lost our appetite; we never see anything but this manna!"

⁷The manna was like coriander seed and looked like resin. ⁸The people went around gathering it, and then ground it in a handmill or crushed it in a mortar. They cooked it in a pot or made it into cakes. And it tasted like something made with olive oil. ⁹When the dew settled on the camp at night, the manna also came down.

¹⁰Moses heard the people of every family wailing, each at the entrance to his tent. The LORD became exceedingly angry, and Moses was troubled. ¹¹He asked the LORD, "Why have you brought this trouble on your servant? What have I done to displease you that you put the burden of all these people on me? ¹²Did I conceive all these people? Did I give them birth? Why do you tell me to carry them in my arms, as a nurse carries an infant, to the land you promised on oath to their forefathers? ¹³Where can I get meat for all these people? They keep wailing to me, 'Give us meat to eat!' ¹⁴I cannot carry all these people by myself; the burden is too heavy for me. ¹⁵If this is how you are going to treat me, put me to death right now — if I have found favor in your eyes — and do not let me face my own ruin."

A second complaint originated with the mixed multitude or "rabble" which was traveling with the Israelites. Apparently there were some Egyptians who had married Israelites and had decided to travel with the children of Israel to the Promised Land. The content of the complaint was the supposed inadequacy of the manna, the miracle food God provided for his wandering people each day. The people wanted meat and vegetables. The desire in itself was not wrong, but the attitude of complaint led the people to remember the tantalizing tastes of the treats Egypt had to offer. How quickly the Israelites forgot the whole situation! How could they claim that the food in Egypt was "at no cost"? How could they so quickly ignore the bitter burden of bondage that they had endured in Egyptian slavery?

To provide a balanced picture Moses inserts a paragraph about manna. He also describes the different ways in which it was prepared. Most important of all, it was there each morning with the dew. (For more about manna, especially in its raw form see Exodus 16:31-35.) Though manna did not suit everyone's taste, it was a very adequate food.

The complaint spread through the entire camp. Moses could hear the people as they sat in front of their tents and wailed. He also became aware that the Lord was angry. He felt like the person in the middle. Though being in the middle is the natural place for a mediator, the lament of Moses focused on the fact that it seemed impossible for him to direct and lead this particular people. But there was more — why had the Lord put such an impossible burden on him? Why should he be held responsible, since he had not produced the nation? How could he produce meat for them, as they seemed to expect of him? Why not just end his life now rather than allow him to be killed by inches?

As heart-rending as the complaint of Moses was, it was still also a prayer for deliverance. In the words "if I have found favor in your eyes," Moses was praying as our Savior did when he said, "Not my will, but thine, be done." Such prayer the Lord gladly answers.

Seventy Elders and the Promise of Meat

16The Lord said to Moses: "Bring me seventy of Israel's elders who are known to you as leaders and officials among the people. Have them come to the Tent of Meeting, that they may stand there with you. 17I will come down and speak with you there, and I will take of the Spirit that is on you and put the Spirit on them. They will help you carry the burden of the people so that you will not have to carry it alone.

18"Tell the people: 'Consecrate yourselves in preparation for tomorrow, when you will eat meat. The Lord heard you when you wailed, "If only we had meat to eat! We were better off in Egypt!" Now the Lord will give you meat, and you will eat it.

¹⁹You will not eat it for just one day, or two days, or five, ten or twenty days, ²⁰but for a whole month — until it comes out of your nostrils and you loathe it — because you have rejected the LORD, who is among you, and have wailed before him, saying, "Why did we ever leave Egypt?" ' "

²¹But Moses said, "Here I am among six hundred thousand men on foot, and you say, 'I will give them meat to eat for a whole month!' ²²Would they have enough if flocks and herds were slaughtered for them? Would they have enough if all the fish in the sea were caught for them?"

²³The LORD answered Moses, "Is the LORD's arm too short? You will now see whether or not what I say will come true for you."

²⁴So Moses went out and told the people what the LORD had said. He brought together seventy of their elders and had them stand around the Tent. ²⁵Then the LORD came down in the cloud and spoke with him, and he took of the Spirit that was on him and put the Spirit on the seventy elders. When the Spirit rested on them, they prophesied, but they did not do so again.

²⁶However, two men, whose names were Eldad and Medad, had remained in the camp. They were listed among the elders, but did not go out to the Tent. Yet the Spirit also rested on them, and they prophesied in the camp. ²⁷A young man ran and told Moses, "Eldad and Medad are prophesying in the camp."

²⁸Joshua son of Nun, who had been Moses' aide since youth, spoke up and said, "Moses, my lord, stop them!"

²⁹But Moses replied, "Are you jealous for my sake? I wish that all the LORD's people were prophets and that the LORD would put his Spirit on them!" ³⁰Then Moses and the elders of Israel returned to the camp.

In answer to Moses' prayer, the Lord addressed the needs of Moses first and proceeded to provide help. Seventy elders, who were known to be responsible leaders, were to be selected. Their responsibility would be to help Moses in the administration of the nation. On them the Lord would put his Spirit.

Through this decision Moses had the needed assistance and he felt the relief immediately. Today too the Lord gives understanding and wisdom to the men that are holding offices in the church. May the Lord lead them with a proper meekness to serve him in all things!

Then the Lord announced that the people were to consecrate themselves for the next day, because they would have meat to eat. The meat would be so bountiful that they would eat meat for a whole month. In fact, it would be so bountiful that it would seem that they had too much meat. They would feel that it was coming out of their nostrils and it would become repulsive to them.

The promise of God's bounty took Moses' breath away. Should the flocks and herds be used to satisfy this whim of the people? Why, it seemed that even all the fish of the sea would not be enough to feed so large a nation. Moses reacted in the same way that Jesus' disciples did. They offered the Savior the loaves and fishes to feed the 5,000 men, and asked, "But how far will they go among so many?" (John 6:9).

To Moses' questions the Lord merely answers, "Is the LORD's arm too short?" that is, "Is the LORD's power limited?" What a pointed reminder that we should not underestimate the Lord and his power. In a very abrupt way Moses, who had emphasized the "I" so much in his complaint, is reminded to look to the Lord for deliverance. Moses was to experience — once again — that the Lord will keep his Word, even when it comes to providing vast amounts of food for a great nation.

Moses then proceeded to select the seventy elders. They were instructed to present themselves at the Tent of Meeting the next morning.

In the morning the presence of the Lord became evident in the cloud of light/fire, which settled over the tabernacle.

Then, as promised, the Spirit was put upon the elders. This was an extension of the work of the Spirit, rather than a partitioning of the Spirit. One Bible scholar has used the happy comparison that it was like lighting seventy candles from one candle. In such a procedure an extension of the fire and light is accomplished without diminishing the light of the first candle. When the men received the Spirit, they began to prophesy, that is, they began to proclaim the Word of the Lord.

For some unknown reason Eldad and Medad, two of the men selected, had not presented themselves at the Tabernacle. They, however, began prophesying (that is, preaching or proclaiming) in the camp. Some, including Joshua, felt that the two men should be stopped. Moses, however, responded that he wished the whole people would receive the Spirit.

Through these administrative helpers many of Moses' difficulties were solved.

Quail and Death

31 Now a wind went out from the LORD and drove quail in from the sea. It brought them down all around the camp to about three feet above the ground, as far as a day's walk in any direction. 32 All that day and night and all the next day the people went out and gathered quail. No one gathered less than ten homers. Then they spread them out all around the camp. 33 But while the meat was still between their teeth and before it could be consumed, the anger of the LORD burned against the people, and he struck them with a severe plague. 34 Therefore the place was named Kibroth Hattaavah, because there they buried the people who had craved other food.

35 From Kibroth Hattaavah the people traveled to Hazeroth and stayed there.

The Lord did provide the meat which he had promised. His arm was not "too short." At the Lord's direction a wind drove a huge flock of quail to the camps of the Israelites. The quail were so numerous that they lay a day's journey in every direction from the camp. There are two ways of understanding the expression "three feet above the ground." One is that the quail were piled three feet deep. Or it is quite possible that the wind from the Lord drove the quail close enough to the ground — "three feet above the ground" — so the Israelites could easily catch them.

In either case, an astounding quantity of meat was available. The people greedily gathered baskets full of quail. No one gathered less than sixty bushels! Some they ate; then they laid some of it out to dry, planning to enjoy the meat at a later time.

Then the Lord's punishment struck. While the meat was still in their mouths, the Lord sent a plague. Many died from the plague.

Obviously the whole nation did not die. In some cases the deaths may have been caused by greediness. Yet the Lord was clearly acting in punishment. Did the plague strike only those who were the complainers? Did it also strike any who had failed to consecrate themselves? Had some focused their attentions so completely on their complaints? We don't know. Yet the Lord acted in a clear way to show his displeasure with the fact that the people had been complaining bitterly and had downgraded the blessings that he had provided. The punishment of the Lord was so severe that the place was named Kibroth Hattaavah, which means "Graves of Greediness." The "Graves of Greediness" should be a constant warning to us that it is easy to accept our food from the Lord with such casualness that it is virtually an insult to the Lord.

A final note indicates that the children of Israel moved on to Hazeroth.

The Next Problem

12 Miriam and Aaron began to talk against Moses because of his Cushite wife, for he had married a Cushite. ²"Has the LORD spoken only through Moses?" they asked. "Hasn't he also spoken through us?" And the LORD heard this.

³(Now Moses was a very humble man, more humble than anyone else on the face of the earth.)

The biblical accounts concentrate on events that show progression in the spiritual condition of the Israelites rather than on giving a complete list of events in chronological order. As they set out from Sinai their spiritual condition began to go downhill. We can observe a progressive rebelliousness against the Lord in the events that are recorded. At Kibroth-Hattaavah the people were dissatisfied because of the food God was providing. A more serious decline occurs at Hazeroth where the Scriptures report a case of disloyalty and rebelliousness.

What a jolt for Moses! The first seeds of mutiny arose from within his own family. Miriam his sister and Aaron his brother challenged Moses' position as the sole leader of the people.

Miriam seems to have been the instigator. Two points in the text support such a conclusion. In Hebrew a man would usually be named before a woman. Yet here Miriam is named first. The second point is that the Hebrew verb has a feminine form. A literal translation would reveal this emphasis by saying: "Miriam and Aaron, she began to talk. . . ." Aaron, as the oldest brother, seems to have followed his sister's lead quite willingly. Again it seems that Aaron's backbone was not as stiff as it should have been. This flaw in his character was also obvious when the people had requested the golden calf. Then he was weak-kneed and gave in to them. In this situation also he rode the fence and displayed a lack of conviction and courage.

The substance of the attack on Moses was two-pronged. One attack questioned whether Moses was worthy of leadership, since he had married inappropriately. Miriam and Aaron attacked Moses through his wife, calling her a Cushite woman. This term is probably best interpreted as an ethnic slur, a "below the belt" attack all too common even today. In the emotional heat of the situation Miriam and Aaron were not very careful about the truth of their attack. Zipporah, whose marriage to Moses is reported in Exodus 2:21, would more appropriately be called a Midianitess. If a person feels compelled to reconcile this difference, it can also be done through the geneaological table in Genesis 10 and 11, where we are told that part of the family of Cush settled in the Sinai Peninsula. Consequently the strains of Cushite blood might have been coursing in Zipporah's veins.

For the first time we encounter the ethnic pride of the Israelites. This is the first example of contempt for other nations. Unfortunately, such an attitude appeared again and again throughout Israel's history. Because the people lost sight of the fact that God had acted in grace when he selected them, their attitude became one of ethnic pride, not the proper pride in being God's treasured people, who would bear the Savior.

The real reason for their attack, however, seems to have been the office of Moses. The emphasis was on the word "only." Miriam's claim to leadership was based on the fact that she was called as a prophetess in Exodus 15:20. This title was assigned to her when she led the women of Israel in a song of exaltation after Israel had been delivered at the Red Sea. Aaron's claim was based on the fact that he, Moses' older brother, was the High Priest and the Lord had revealed himself to Aaron and had also spoken to him. On these grounds Miriam and Aaron claimed that the Lord had "spoken through us also." They wanted equality with Moses, their younger brother.

The jealousy had surfaced!

Verse 3 presents a problem in that Moses, the author of Numbers, is described as the humblest of men. On the surface it seems that Moses is describing a humility that is proud of itself. Isn't it an obvious contradiction for Moses to be proudly humble? The answer, of course, lies in the fact that the Holy Spirit caused these words to be written. This statement is the Lord's stamp of approval on Moses. The Lord considered it appropriate to mention the humility of Moses at this point, because Moses did not retaliate against his brother and sister. God's chosen leader was willing to wait for the Lord to provide the solution to the problem.

An alternate but inferior solution lies in a possible meaning of the Hebrew word that is here translated as "humble." Some translators take the word to mean "afflicted, troubled, plagued or miserable." Thoughts about affliction and trouble surely fit very well at this moment in the life of Moses. But this translation forces the word away from its primary meaning.

The Lord himself was quick to intervene on behalf of his chosen servant:

The Lord Called a Hearing

⁴At once the LORD said to Moses, Aaron and Miriam, "Come out to the Tent of Meeting, all three of you." So the three of them came out. ⁵Then the LORD came down in a pillar of cloud; he stood at the entrance to the Tent and summoned Aaron and Miriam. When both of them stepped forward, ⁶he said, "Listen to my words:

"When a prophet of the LORD is among you,
    I reveal myself to him in visions,
    I speak to him in dreams.

> [7]But this is not true of my servant Moses;
>   he is faithful in all my house.
> [8]With him I speak face to face,
>   clearly and not in riddles;
>   he sees the form of the LORD.
>   Why then were you not afraid
>   to speak against my servant Moses?"
> [9]The anger of the LORD burned against them, and he left them.

The Lord acted decisively to resolve the problem. He issued an immediate summons.

When Moses, Aaron and Miriam gathered at the tabernacle, the Lord appeared in the cloud of his presence. Yet, because he revealed his presence only in the cloud, there was already a hint of judgment. Further, the Lord presented himself at the doorway of the Tent of Meeting. Miriam could not even enter the Holy Place of the tabernacle, much less the Most Holy Place where God normally talked with Moses. Therefore the Lord met them outside between the altar and the Tent of Meeting.

No witnesses were necessary. The Lord knew every word that had been spoken. He addressed Aaron and Miriam immediately and directly. There was no doubt that the Lord intended to vindicate Moses completely. He made three points. First, it is the Lord, not human beings, who chooses prophets by giving them visions and dreams. Secondly, the Lord stated that Moses had been given a position that was superior to all other prophets. The fact that he spoke to Moses face to face demonstrated Moses' superiority (Deuteronomy 34:10). On many occasions the Lord communicated to Moses in a conversational way, openly and not in dark sayings. Another aspect of the superiority of Moses was the privilege of beholding the form of the Lord. From the time of the burning bush the Lord had come frequently to speak to Moses. Especially on Mount Sinai and in the

Tent of Meeting the Lord had revealed his presence to Moses again and again.

The third point was a direct indictment of the mutiny. Miriam and Aaron were guilty. They were getting far more than they bargained for. Though they thought they were attacking the man Moses they were really rebelling against the Lord himself. He claimed Moses as "my servant." By discrediting his servant they were directly challenging God's wisdom and rights. How clearly and powerfully the Lord showed that he stood behind the statement, "He that rejects you, rejects me; and he who rejects me rejects him who sent me" (Luke 10:16).

The case was closed! Miriam and Aaron had no opportunity for explanations, excuses or objections. There was no need for a cross-examination. The all-knowing Lord knew the facts; he had had his say; and so he departed.

The Lord Acted in Judgment and Mercy

10 When the cloud lifted from above the Tent, there stood Miriam — leprous, like snow. Aaron turned toward her and saw that she had leprosy; 11 and he said to Moses, "Please, my lord, do not hold against us the sin we have so foolishly committed. 12 Do not let her be like a stillborn infant coming from its mother's womb with its flesh half eaten away."

13 So Moses cried out to the LORD, "O God, please heal her!"

14 The LORD replied to Moses, "If her father had spit in her face, would she not have been in disgrace for seven days? Confine her outside the camp for seven days; after that she can be brought back." 15 So Miriam was confined outside the camp for seven days, and the people did not move on till she was brought back.

16 After that, the people left Hazeroth and encamped in the Desert of Paran.

The Lord acted sternly and immediately against this rebelliousness. The sentence was immediately carried out.

Miriam became leprous. She alone was afflicted. This fact provides further support for the conclusion drawn earlier that she was the chief instigator of the rebellion.

When Aaron noticed the illness of his sister, he directed a plea to Moses. Through the words "my lord" Aaron showed that he was again willing to submit to Moses as God's chosen mediator. Therefore his own position was subordinate. This time the actions and words of Aaron are a clear improvement over his actions at the time of the golden calf. Then Aaron tried to pass the buck to the people. At this point he used the words "sinned . . . acted foolishly . . . sinned." These words have the ring of true repentance. The argumentativeness has been drained from Aaron. His only plea is for mercy — let the terrible punishment be removed from Miriam. Don't let her be like a half-decayed, stillborn child.

In response to Aaron's pleas Moses again acted as mediator on behalf of his brother and sister. He addressed a simple prayer to the Lord on behalf of Miriam. The Lord answered the prayer. And in so doing God in a very emphatic way put his stamp of approval on Moses as his mediator. Even as the Lord acted in mercy, he qualified that mercy by stating that there was really no reason for leniency. Among the Israelites even a human father who had spit on a rebellious daughter would have her excluded from the camp for seven days. Should the Lord do less to this rebellious daughter? Though the Lord could have acted more severely, he allowed the chastisement to be shortened to a seven day exclusion from the camp. Such an exclusion was very appropriate, because Miriam had really suffered from leprosy. Though the Lord in his goodness immediately healed Miriam, the requirement would still be made that she follow the normal procedure for cleansed lepers. She would be excluded from the camp for seven days. After that time the priest could examine her and declare her clean. Only then would she be allowed to return to normal life in the camp.

Yet the goodness of the Lord is evident in another way. He did not lift up the cloud from the tabernacle during the seven days of Miriam's exclusion from the camp. Miriam's woes would have been infinitely greater if the Lord had led the people away, leaving her behind.

What a vivid lesson in humility! It was true that the Lord had used Miriam as a prophetess. He had also called Aaron as High Priest. They should have recognized that the assignment to such functions was already an act of grace on God's part. How thankful they should have been for the privilege! How easily God could have put them to shame! He could have removed them from office. In a moment he could even remove them from his chosen people through leprosy. As severe and sudden as the chastisement was, the mercy and goodness of the Lord is even more remarkable. He allowed Miriam to continue in fellowship with his people. Miriam was actually blessed by this act of chastisement as she realized the measure of God's grace to her. How wonderful his mercy!

For all ages God himself is the judge between his servants and those who dare to flaunt their own notions before him. It will always be a dangerous thing to challenge the authority of those who have the Word of God on their side!

Sending the Spies and Their Instructions

13 The Lord said to Moses, ²"Send some men to explore the land of Canaan, which I am giving to the Israelites. From each ancestral tribe send one of its leaders."

³So at the Lord's command Moses sent them out from the Desert of Paran. All of them were leaders of the Israelites. ⁴These are their names:

from the tribe of Reuben, Shammua son of Zaccur;
⁵from the tribe of Simeon, Shaphat son of Hori;
⁶from the tribe of Judah, Caleb son of Jephunneh;
⁷from the tribe of Issachar, Igal son of Joseph;
⁸from the tribe of Ephraim, Hoshea son of Nun;
⁹from the tribe of Benjamin, Palti son of Raphu;
¹⁰from the tribe of Zebulun, Gaddiel son of Sodi;
¹¹from the tribe of Manasseh (a tribe of Joseph), Gaddi son
    of Susi;
¹²from the tribe of Dan, Ammiel son of Gemalli;
¹³from the tribe of Asher, Sethur son of Michael;
¹⁴from the tribe of Naphtali, Nahbi son of Vophsi;
¹⁵from the tribe of Gad, Geuel son of Maki.

¹⁶These are the names of the men Moses sent to explore the land. (Moses gave Hoshea son of Nun the name Joshua.)

¹⁷When Moses sent them to explore Canaan, he said, "Go up through the Negev and on into the hill country. ¹⁸See what the land is like and whether the people who live there are strong or weak, few or many. ¹⁹What kind of land do they live in? Is it good or bad? What kind of towns do they live in? Are they unwalled or fortified? ²⁰How is the soil? Is it fertile or poor? Are there trees on it or not? Do your best to bring back some of the fruit of the land." (It was the season for the first ripe grapes.)

Sounds of the events recorded in the next two chapters echo and re-echo through all the later history of Israel. The immediate aftermath of the rebellion at Kadesh-barnea was the wandering in the wilderness, but references to the sojourn in the wilderness recur through the entire Old Testament and into the New Testament.

The issue was simple: Would the people proceed into the Promised Land on the basis of faith in the Lord's strength and goodness? Or would they be deceived by what was visible to their eyes? Stated another way, the question was: Would doubt lead them to question God's promises and accept Satan's siren song, "Did God really say, . . . ?" (Genesis 3:1)

The case in favor of proceeding on faith was substantial. They had been delivered from the Egyptians by God's mighty hand. They had arrived at Kadesh-barnea, even though at first they had been led south to the Red Sea and Mount Sinai. The Lord had sustained them by manna and on occasion had provided meat. A miraculous victory had been given them over the Amalekites. The Lord had favored them by revealing his Law and Covenant. The tabernacle had been consecrated and the priesthood had been established in their midst. They had an outstanding leader and mediator in the person of Moses. Again and again the Lord had promised that they would be going to the "land that I will give you."

But the moment of truth was at hand. Would they now proceed with confidence in the promises of the Lord or would they evaluate on the basis of their own human judgment and ability?

When Moses recounted these events in Deuteronomy 1:19-25 he reported that the request to send out spies had originated with the people. They wanted to know what route to take and the nature of the cities. Apparently Moses followed his usual procedure when considering such a request from the people. He had consulted the Lord, for the text in Deuteronomy introduces God's statement of permission with the words: "The LORD said to Moses." But when the Lord gave the instruction to send out the spies, he included the promise that the land of Canaan was the land that "I am giving to the Israelites." The Lord's pledge had been given! He was going to bring success! Sending spies was only for the sake of the people! God didn't need them!

So the spies were selected according to the Lord's instruction. One was chosen from each tribe. After the selections were made, Moses gave them detailed instructions. They were to examine the entire country from the south (Negev) to the north (Lebo Hamath). They were to see whether the land was good or bad, whether the people were strong or weak, many or few. They were to examine the cities to determine whether the people lived in camps or in settlements surrounded by walls. They were also to make an effort to bring back some fruit of the land.

None of these directions was inappropriate, even if the people went forward with confidence in the Lord. For if they went forward in faith, the information which the spies had gathered would exalt the Lord. God was giving them the land. In his power they would overcome even the most powerful inhabitants. So the greater the foe, the more the Lord would be exalted in granting victory. The more precise and complete the information, the more clearly the blessing of the Lord could be seen.

The Spying and the Report

[21] So they went up and explored the land from the Desert of Zin as far as Rehob, toward Lebo Hamath. [22] They went up through the Negev and came to Hebron, where Ahiman, Sheshai and Talmai, the descendants of Anak, lived. (Hebron had been built seven years before Zoan in Egypt.) [23] When they reached the Valley of Eshcol, they cut off a branch bearing a single cluster of grapes. Two of them carried it on a pole between them, along with some pomegranates and figs. [24] That place was called the Valley of Eshcol because of the cluster of grapes the Israelites cut off there. [25] At the end of forty days they returned from exploring the land.

[26] They came back to Moses and Aaron and the whole Israelite community at Kadesh in the Desert of Paran. There they reported to them and to the whole assembly and showed them the fruit of the land. [27] They gave Moses this account: "We went into the land to which you sent us, and it does flow with milk and honey! Here

The Grapes of Canaan

is its fruit. ²⁸But the people who live there are powerful, and the cities are fortified and very large. We even saw descendants of Anak there. ²⁹The Amalekites live in the Negev; the Hittites, Jebusites and Amorites live in the hill country; and the Canaanites live near the sea and along the Jordan."

³⁰Then Caleb silenced the people before Moses and said, "We should go up and take possession of the land, for we can certainly do it."

³¹But the men who had gone up with him said, "We can't attack those people; they are stronger than we are." ³²And they spread among the Israelites a bad report about the land they had explored. They said, "The land we explored devours those living in it. All people we saw there are of great size. ³³We saw the Nephilim there (the descendants of Anak come from the Nephilim). We seemed like grasshoppers in our own eyes, and we looked the same to them."

The spies followed their orders carefully. Their course spanned the whole land from the wilderness of Zin in the south to the far north (Rehob and Lebo Hamath). They also examined special areas like Hebron the home of the Anakim (who apparently were very tall), and the valley of Eschol where they obtained a large cluster of grapes.

After forty days the spies returned and made their report before Moses and the people. The majority report was: The land is indeed good as the fruit we brought back shows. "But": (1) The people are strong. (2) The cities are fortified. (3) The people are fierce (descendants of Anak, Amalekites, Hittites, Jebusites, Amorites and Canaanites).

When Caleb noted the direction that the majority report was taking, he intervened. Looking beyond the mere factual data, he urged: "Go up. Take possession. We shall surely overcome." Boldly Caleb encouraged the people to go forward with full confidence in the Lord's promise and power.

But the majority rebutted: "We are not able." "They are too strong." "The land devours its inhabitants." (Apparently they meant that it was a country surrounded by fierce nations who were in a constant state of warfare for its possession.) "They are the Nephilim and we were as grasshoppers in our own sight and theirs."

The majority report was correct when it used the "We" saying, "WE are not able." They could not conquer the land in their own strength. However, they erred by ignoring the Lord's promise to Israel. They also forgot that they were God's instruments to bring judgment down upon the peoples of Canaan who had filled up the cup of God's wrath to the brim.

In God's sight the Anakim were as grasshoppers. He could give Israel total victory. That special factor was ignored by the majority.

Unfortunately the majority report prevailed. So this incident stands as a warning to the church in all ages. Majorities opposing or ignoring God's Word are always wrong. Unfortunately all too often such majority opinion prevails.

The crucial moment had come! The nation failed at this point and became a picture of the future generation which also failed to recognize its blessing and source of strength. And just as Moses' generation in their unbelief refused to enter that land of promise, rebelling against God and Moses, even so a later generation would reject the Savior. They would turn their back on Christ Jesus, disowning him and crying, "Away with him! Crucify him!"

In all ages matters have reached an unfortunate stage in the church when those who are called to be leaders of the congregation cannot distinguish spiritual light from spiritual darkness. How sad it is when the leaders lose courage and dread the battle with the powers of Satan. But God always has some witnesses and servants who encourage his people and proclaim the promise of certain victory with the help of the Lord. May simple Christians always conscientiously choose to follow those who are acting on the basis of God's Word!

The People Rebel

14 **That night all the people of the community raised their voices and wept aloud. ²All the Israelites grumbled against Moses and Aaron, and the whole assembly said to them, "If only we had died in Egypt! Or in this desert! ³Why is the LORD bringing us to this land only to let us fall by the sword? Our wives and children will be taken as plunder. Wouldn't it be better for us to go back to Egypt?" ⁴And they said to each other, "We should choose a leader and go back to Egypt."**

⁵Then Moses and Aaron fell facedown in front of the whole Israelite assembly gathered there. ⁶Joshua son of Nun and Caleb son of Jephunneh, who were among those who had explored the land, tore their clothes ⁷and said to the entire Israelite assembly, "The land we passed through and explored is exceedingly good. ⁸If the LORD is pleased with us, he will lead us into that land, a land flowing with milk and honey, and will give it to us. ⁹Only do not rebel against the LORD. And do not be afraid of the people of the land, because we will swallow them up. Their protection is gone, but the LORD is with us. Do not be afraid of them."

¹⁰But the whole assembly talked about stoning them.

All that night the people wept because they believed the majority report of the spies. In the morning they grumbled against Moses and Aaron. More significantly they were rebelling against the LORD. The oft-repeated lament of the people echoed through the camp: If only we had died in Egypt or in the wilderness! Their feelings were so negative that they assumed that everything would go wrong if they entered the land of Canaan. Had Moses brought them there so that they would fall by the sword? Wouldn't their wives and children become plunder?

It is interesting to note how their sinful fears produce gross exaggeration. Defeat is a foregone conclusion. "All" the people are bigger and stronger. The cities are fortified to the sky! (Deuteronomy 1:28)

In answer to these fears Moses had patiently pointed to the true Leader of Israel: The LORD will fight on your behalf (Deuteronomy 1:30). All their experiences supported confidence in the Lord. He had delivered them from hopeless situations in Egypt. He had provided his support in the wilderness. In words that could not be misunderstood, Moses also pointed to the nub of the problem: "You did not trust the LORD" (Deuteronomy 1:32).

The scene also shows Joshua and Caleb forcefully urging the minority report. Their grief and dismay is evident as they tear their clothes. "If the LORD is pleased with us, he will lead us into that land . . . and will give it to us. Only do not rebel against the LORD." Moreover, Joshua and Caleb pointed out that the people of the land would be the Israelites' prey: "Their protection is gone, but the LORD is with us."

The Lord is with us — how well this serves as the theme for the whole book of Numbers. Here it stands at this crucial point in the history of Israel. The evidence of the past was clear and unassailable. The witness of Moses, Caleb and Joshua was persuasive. The moment is poised as it were on the edge of a sword, ready to bring blessing upon obedience, but just as surely bringing the Lord's chastisement for disobedience.

But the decision had been made. In their fear and unbelief the people became surly. They turned on the faithful leaders and seriously considered stoning the very ones who were urging them to go forward with confidence in the Lord.

Since they turned from the promises of the Lord they brought on themselves the judgment expressed later in this chapter: "I will do to you the very thing I heard you say . . . you will know what it is like to have me against you" (Numbers 14:28,34).

We have here a picture of the manner in which unbelievers reject the proofs of God's goodness and mercy and repudiate the warnings and admonitions of God's faithful witnesses. But God will not be mocked. According to his plan his judgments come upon the world with impressive exhibitions of his might.

The Lord Is Ready to Act in Judgment

Then the glory of the LORD appeared at the Tent of Meeting to all the Israelites. ¹¹The LORD said to Moses, "How long will these people treat me with contempt? How long will they refuse to believe in me, in spite of all the miraculous signs I have performed among them? ¹²I will strike them down with a plague and destroy them, but I will make you into a nation greater and stronger than they."

The Lord's patience with the people had been exhausted. He appeared in the special manifestation of his glory that he used when he spoke with Moses. His chief criticism of the people was: "How long will they refuse to believe in me, in spite of the miraculous signs I have performed among them?" The Lord was ready to act in a way that would punish the people, but would still accomplish his great purposes for the world. "I will strike them down with a plague and destroy them, but I will make you (Moses) into a nation greater and stronger than they."

Moses' Prayer on Behalf of the People

¹³Moses said to the LORD, "Then the Egyptians will hear about it! By your power you brought these people up from among them.

¹⁴And they will tell the inhabitants of this land about it. They have already heard that you, O LORD, are with these people and that you, O LORD, have been seen face to face, that your cloud stays over them, and that you go before them in a pillar of cloud by day and a pillar of fire by night. ¹⁵If you put these people to death all at one time, the nations who have heard this report about you will say, ¹⁶'The LORD was not able to bring these people into the land he promised them on oath; so he slaughtered them in the desert.'

¹⁷"Now may the LORD's strength be displayed, just as you have declared: ¹⁸'The LORD is slow to anger, abounding in love and forgiving sin and rebellion. Yet he does not leave the guilty unpunished; he punishes the children for the sin of the fathers to the third and fourth generation.' ¹⁹In accordance with your great love, forgive the sin of these people, just as you have pardoned them from the time they left Egypt until now."

At this point, though the temptation to personal advantage was presented to Moses, this faithful servant remained true to his God-given call as the mediator and intercessor for the people. His prayer on behalf of the people could only repeat the same arguments that he had used when the people had sinned in worshipping the golden calf. In both cases he acted properly as a mediator and acted on behalf of the people he served rather than for personal gain. Such mediation is truly a beautiful picture that prefigures the attitude and work of Christ, the great Mediator between man and God.

Moses pointed out first that the Lord's glory was at stake. The nations had heard that the Lord was in the midst of this people, that he appeared face to face with Moses and that the cloud of his presence traveled with the Israelites. If the Lord now destroyed this nation, other nations would say, "He was not able to bring this people to the land he promised them on oath." Such a conclusion would certainly discredit the Lord.

The second plea was directed to the loving kindness of the Lord. Such a plea for God's grace is ultimately the basis of every prayer that comes before him. God's steadfast love was the only hope of the people, especially in view of their sinfulness and rebellion. Drawing on God's own proclamation about his holy name in Exodus 34, Moses pleaded, "Forgive the sin of these people . . . just as you have pardoned them from the time they left Egypt until now." Here is the basis of effective prayer: it takes hold of the Word and promises of the Lord and will not relent until it is answered.

The Lord's Decision

20The LORD replied, "I have forgiven them, as you asked. 21Nevertheless, as surely as I live and as surely as the glory of the LORD fills the whole earth, 22not one of the men who saw my glory and the miraculous signs I performed in Egypt and in the desert but who disobeyed me and tested me ten times — 23not one of them will ever see the land I promised on oath to their forefathers. No one who has treated me with contempt will ever see it. 24But because my servant Caleb has a different spirit and follows me wholeheartedly, I will bring him into the land he went to, and his descendants will inherit it. 25Since the Amalekites and Canaanites are living in the valleys, turn back tomorrow and set out toward the desert along the route to the Red Sea."

26The LORD said to Moses and Aaron: 27"How long will this wicked community grumble against me? I have heard the complaints of these grumbling Israelites. 28So tell them, 'As surely as I live, declares the LORD, I will do to you the very things I heard you say: 29In this desert your bodies will fall — every one of you twenty years old or more who was counted in the census and who has grumbled against me. 30Not one of you will enter the land I swore with uplifted hand to make your home, except Caleb son of Jephunneh and Joshua son of Nun. 31As for your children that you said would be taken as plunder, I will bring them in to enjoy the land you have rejected. 32But you — your bodies will fall in

this desert. ³³Your children will be shepherds here for forty years,
suffering for your unfaithfulness, until the last of your bodies lies
in the desert. ³⁴For forty years — one year for each of the forty
days you explored the land — you will suffer for your sins and
know what it is like to have me against you.' ³⁵I, the LORD, have
spoken, and I will surely do these things to this whole wicked
community, which has banded together against me. They will
meet their end in this desert; here they will die."

The Lord addressed the last plea of Moses first: "I have
forgiven. I will not destroy them. Indeed all the earth will be
filled with my glory, even as I now chastise this generation
and ultimately carry out my purposes. But there will be
chastisement. The men who have seen my glory and my
signs, and who yet have tested me these ten times shall by no
means see the land. The only exceptions to this chastisement
will be Caleb and Joshua" (Numbers 14:24,30).

Before giving additional details of the chastisement, the
Lord takes a solemn oath that he will carry out the judgment
(verse 28). (This oath was repeated many times in Ezekiel,
when another judgment of the Lord was impending.) The
faithless conclusion of those who stated they would die in
the wilderness, rather than go up to Canaan, will be accom-
modated. "Your corpses shall fall in the wilderness" (verse
32). But the lament that their children would be a prey
would not come true. In those children the glory and power
of the Lord would be magnified, as he preserved the nation.

He would also bring those very children victoriously into
the Promised Land, even though they had appeared so
vulnerable to the doubters. The children, suffering for the
unfaithfulness of their fathers, would be shepherds or
wanderers in the wilderness for forty years. Each year of the
forty years was to match one of the forty days that the spies
had examined the land.

An Immediate Judgment Is Carried Out

³⁶So the men Moses had sent to explore the land, who returned and made the whole community grumble against him by spreading a bad report about it — ³⁷these men responsible for spreading the bad report about the land were struck down and died of a plague before the LORD. ³⁸Of the men who went to explore the land, only Joshua son of Nun and Caleb son of Jephunneh survived.

The judgment of the Lord was not yet finished. The ten spies who had submitted the negative majority report "died of the plague before the LORD." God's judgment on the fearful spies was immediate. How serious the responsibility of those who are given leadership positions among the people of God!

The hand of the Lord was evident in a double way. Not only were those who advised against going to Canaan struck down, but both Caleb and Joshua, who had urged, "The LORD is with us," were spared. In this way the Lord showed the seriousness of the rebellion. At the same time he showed with certainty that he would carry out the further chastisements that he had described. Yet the message was also loud and clear that he would bless those who believed that he was with this people.

A Complete Reversal

³⁹When Moses reported this to all the Israelites, they mourned bitterly. ⁴⁰Early the next morning they went up toward the high hill country. "We have sinned," they said. "We will go up to the place the LORD promised."

⁴¹But Moses said, "Why are you disobeying the LORD's command? This will not succeed! ⁴²Do not go up, because the LORD is not with you. You will be defeated by your enemies, ⁴³for the Amalekites and Canaanites will face you there. Because you have

turned away from the LORD, he will not be with you and you will fall by the sword."

⁴⁴Nevertheless, in their presumption they went up toward the high hill country, though neither Moses nor the ark of the LORD's covenant moved from the camp. ⁴⁵Then the Amalekites and Canaanites who lived in that hill country came down and attacked them and beat them down all the way to Hormah.

What a change a day makes! The Israelites realized that they would certainly have obtained the land, had they gone forward with the Lord. Yesterday the land of promise was so close! Today it was lost to them! Not one of the adults would ever enter it! But if they had done wrong yesterday, they reasoned, let's do the opposite today. Surely the opposite then must be the right thing to do. But in the change of attitude they showed just as surely as in the original rebellion that they did not realize one must seek the Lord when he may be found. So they moved from unbelieving despair to foolhardy presumption.

Blindly the people made a complete reversal. Sullen rebels were suddenly eager and enthusiastic about taking the land. "We will go up to the place the LORD has promised." What a difference one day appears to have made. Now those who earlier refused to go in the strength of the Lord were ready to go up in their own strength without the Lord! They persisted in their plan even though Moses warned them, "You will fall by the sword."

When the people persisted, they went without the Lord, without Moses and without the ark of the covenant. What a commentary this is on the power of sin! The Scriptures tell us that they went out "heedlessly" (verse 44) and "presumptuously" (Deuteronomy 1:43). This sham obedience was not based on simple faith in the Lord's promise. It was a confidence in self and in reality only another form of unbelief. Remorse and repentance may be hard to distinguish until they lead to action. Then remorse becomes as self-willed as the action from which it arose, while repentance before God leads to new obedience to him.

To chastise Israel in these circumstances, the Lord did not need to use his miraculous power. When the people went out without his hand and protection, the Amalekites and Canaanites were perfectly capable of doing the very things that the people had feared. A resounding defeat followed! The rout extended from Seir to Hormah. "They chased you like bees do" (Deuteronomy 1:44) was the vivid description that Moses gave the defeat.

How well this illustrates the statement, "Seek the LORD while he may be found; call on him while he is near" (Isaiah 55:6). "Too late" is a sad and almost inadequate way to describe the misguided eagerness of the remorseful Israelites. The previous day they had been taught that their seeming weakness could be real strength, while the Lord was with them. This day they had the bitter experience that their seeming strength was valueless when the Lord was not with them.

The severity of the Lord is plain. He acted with sternness because the Israelites refused his leadership. But his mercy was just as plain for in condemning them to wander in the wilderness until the forty years were finished, he also committed himself to providing for them. He gave them manna through all those years (Exodus 16:35). He kept their clothes from wearing out (Deuteronomy 8:4). He continued to forgive them. He ultimately carried out his promise to bring the children into the Promised Land. That is what the rest of the book of Numbers is all about.

Truly even while they were under God's judgment, it was clear that believers among Israel could still exclaim, "The LORD is with us."

PART II
THE YEARS OF WANDERING

NUMBERS 15—19

The forty years of wandering in the wilderness are treated very briefly in the Bible. There are a few regulations regarding individual worship that the Lord clarified during this period. Actually, however, from the time Israel left Mount Sinai to the time the nation stood poised to enter its homeland, only a few incidents are recorded. And these deal with rebellion against the Lord and his word.

We are told about a Sabbath-breaker, and about the rebellion of Korah. These events are recorded to show that the judgment of the Lord on this people was indeed just.

To show his will regarding the worship life of the children of Israel the Lord put his stamp of approval on Aaron through the miracle of the budding staff. Additional aspects of the worship life were regulations regarding the priests and Levites and the water of cleansing, which was used by those who were ceremonially unclean.

Life as Individuals

The Lord treats the people of the generation that was about to die in the wilderness almost as non-persons. Yet we note his gracious long-range intentions for the nation in the instructions he gives regarding offerings. To revive the people's hope for the Promised Land and to heighten their anticipation God mentioned that the people were to follow these regulations when they "enter the land I [the Lord] am giving you." As an aid to individual worship, the Lord gave a regulation about having tassels on their garments as a reminder of all the commands of the Lord. Between these two sets of instructions was the sad account about the man who by breaking the Sabbath Day incurred God's wrath.

Supplementary Offerings

15 The LORD said to Moses, 2"Speak to the Israelites and say to them: 'After you enter the land I am giving you as a home 3and you present to the LORD offerings made by fire, from the herd or the flock, as an aroma pleasing to the LORD — whether burnt offerings or sacrifices, for special vows or freewill offerings or festival offerings — 4then the one who brings his offering shall present to the LORD a grain offering of a tenth of an ephah of fine flour mixed with a quarter of a hin of oil. 5With each lamb for the burnt offering or the sacrifice, prepare a quarter of a hin of wine as a drink offering.

6" 'With a ram prepare a grain offering of two-tenths of an ephah of fine flour mixed with a third of a hin of oil, 7and a third of a hin of wine as a drink offering. Offer it as an aroma pleasing to the LORD.

8" 'When you prepare a young bull as a burnt offering or sacrifice, for a special vow or a fellowship offering to the LORD, 9bring with the bull a grain offering of three-tenths of an ephah of fine flour mixed with half a hin of oil. 10Also bring half a hin of wine as a drink offering. It will be an offering made by fire, an aroma pleasing to the LORD. 11Each bull or ram, each lamb or young goat, is to be prepared in this manner. 12Do this for each one, for as many as you prepare.

13" 'Everyone who is native-born must do these things in this way when he brings an offering made by fire as an aroma pleasing to the LORD. 14For the generations to come, whenever an alien or anyone else living among you presents an offering made by fire as an aroma pleasing to the LORD, he must do exactly as you do.

¹⁵The community is to have the same rules for you and for the alien living among you; this is a lasting ordinance for the generations to come. You and the alien shall be the same before the LORD: ¹⁶The same laws and regulations will apply both to you and to the alien living among you.' "

¹⁷The LORD said to Moses, ¹⁸"Speak to the Israelites and say to them: 'When you enter the land to which I am taking you ¹⁹and you eat the food of the land, present a portion as an offering to the LORD. ²⁰Present a cake from the first of your ground meal and present it as an offering from the threshing floor. ²¹Throughout the generations to come you are to give this offering to the LORD from the first of your ground meal.' "

In spite of Israel's rebellion the Lord remained faithful to his promise. The previous chapter closed on the harsh note that showed God's judgment on the unfaithful generation and his punishment of their presumptuous attempt to enter the Promised Land. Yet the first words in this chapter really showed the Lord's faithfulness and love: "After you enter the land I am giving you as a home. . . ." The Lord was not going to go back on his promise. There would be a time in the future when the Israelites would enter the Promised Land. Therefore it was appropriate to give directives about the sacrifices that would apply into that promised future.

The directives that the Lord gave at this point focused on the grain, oil and wine offerings which were to be brought with the various types of animal offerings. The simplest way of presenting this is to use a chart:

	flour	oil	wine
1 lamb	$1/10$ ephah	$1/4$ hin	$1/4$ hin
1 ram	$2/10$ ephah	$1/3$ hin	$1/3$ hin
1 bull	$3/10$ ephah	$1/2$ hin	$1/2$ hin

The chart indicates that the offerings of flour, oil and wine were to be proportionate to the size of the animal offering. (An ephah was a dry measure, a basket equal to five-eighths of a bushel. A hin was liquid measure, a pot which held the equivalent of one gallon.)

Another point that needed clarification was that aliens were to obey the same rules as the native-born Israelites. For clarification it should be noted the aliens referred to here were the converts to Judaism, not outright pagans. But note how clearly the Lord puts the converts in the same position as the native-born. Once a person was brought into God's family there were to be no distinctions in the worship of the Lord.

In the final paragraph of this section the Lord's words are again introduced with the promise: "When you enter the land to which I am taking you. . . ." Though there was to be chastisement for the current generation, the Lord would not break his long-range promise to the nation. The specific directive assumes that the Israelites will settle down and do some planting in the Promised Land. At that time the Israelites were to bring an offering of firstfruits from the threshing floor. Through such an offering they would indeed show that they acknowledged that all their blessings came from the Lord. Christians of all ages would do well to remember that the Lord loves firstfruits, not gifts that are "just good enough" or leftovers.

Offerings for Unintentional Sins

22" 'Now if you unintentionally fail to keep any of these commands the LORD gave Moses — 23any of the LORD's commands to you through him, from the day the LORD gave them and continuing through the generations to come — 24and if this is done unintentionally without the community being aware of it, then the whole community is to offer a young bull for a burnt offering

as an aroma pleasing to the LORD, along with its prescribed grain offering and drink offering, and a male goat for a sin offering. ²⁵The priest is to make atonement for the whole Israelite community, and they will be forgiven, for it was not intentional and they have brought to the LORD for their wrong an offering made by fire and a sin offering. ²⁶The whole Israelite community and the aliens living among them will be forgiven, because all the people were involved in the unintentional wrong.

²⁷" 'But if just one person sins unintentionally, he must bring a year-old female goat for a sin offering. ²⁸The priest is to make atonement before the LORD for the one who erred by sinning unintentionally, and when atonement has been made for him, he will be forgiven. ²⁹One and the same law applies to everyone who sins unintentionally, whether he is a native-born Israelite or an alien.

³⁰" 'But anyone who sins defiantly, whether native-born or alien, blasphemes the LORD, and that person must be cut off from his people. ³¹Because he has despised the LORD's word and broken his commands, that person must surely be cut off; his guilt remains on him.' "

The Lord here addressed the reality that sin can be unintentional or intentional. When the sins were unintentional, whether the whole community was guilty or just an individual, the covenant relationship with God could be restored by bringing the appropriate sin offering.

The final paragraph addresses the vital issues regarding sins of defiance. Such intentional or defiant sins presented a very dangerous situation. God did not assign a specific sacrifice to cover this situation. The covenant relationship with God could not be restored by some kind of sacrifice, as long as the defiance continued. The person guilty of defiant sin was to be "cut off," that is, he was to be cut off from fellowship with the people of God. According to Exodus 31:14 and Leviticus 20:2,3 this cutting off was often synonymous with execution.

Sabbath Breaker Stoned

Translated into terms of the New Testament, these directives serve to remind us that when all brotherly admonitions
have no effect, the unrepentant sinner must be cut off from
the Christian congregation by excommunication. Open rebellion against God's Word makes such a person a pagan
and a tax collector (Matthew 18:20). Excommunication is,
however, an act of love, since we are merely stating publicly
the reality that has already occurred through the person's
impenitence. On the other hand, members of Christian con-
gregations dare never forget that they will become partakers
of other men's sins if they permit evil-doing to go on in their
midst unrebuked and do not take the steps prescribed by
God for calling the impenitent sinner to repentance.

The Sabbath-Breaker Put to Death

**32 While the Israelites were in the desert, a man was found
gathering wood on the Sabbath day. 33 Those who found him
gathering wood brought him to Moses and Aaron and the whole
assembly, 34 and they kept him in custody, because it was not clear
what should be done to him. 35 Then the LORD said to Moses, "The
man must die. The whole assembly must stone him outside the
camp." 36 So the assembly took him outside the camp and stoned
him to death, as the LORD commanded Moses.**

The connection between the incident described in this
paragraph and the sins of defiance which are discussed in the
previous paragraph is quite obvious. The Sabbath-breaker
presents an incident in which the rebellion against God is
demonstrated. As one after another of these situations un-
folds, it seems that God is marking this period by the various
ways in which the old generation died in rebellion, leaving
their carcasses in the wilderness.

The situation was simple and clear. A man disobeyed the
command to rest on the Sabbath. He gathered some wood.

He was observed by a number of people, so there was no question about the facts involved. Indeed the witnesses brought him to Moses and Aaron and before the whole assembly.

It was clear that on the Sabbath God forbade his people to do any work. But it was not clear how the Lord wanted the guilty person to be punished. Therefore the Lord gave Moses the answer: the man should be stoned. This sin was put in the same category as blasphemy against God.

Tassels on Garments

37 The LORD said to Moses, 38"Speak to the Israelites and say to them: 'Throughout the generations to come you are to make tassels on the corners of your garments, with a blue cord on each tassel. 39You will have these tassels to look at and so you will remember all the commands of the LORD, that you may obey them and not prostitute yourselves by going after the lusts of your own hearts and eyes. 40Then you will remember to obey all my commands and will be consecrated to your God. 41I am the LORD your God, who brought you out of Egypt to be your God. I am the LORD your God.' "

Recognizing that human beings can easily forget certain important things, the Lord provided that the Israelites should have a reminder that would be with them at all times. They were to make tassels for the corners of their garments. The tassels were to be a constant reminder that they were the people of God. They were also to encourage the people to live a devout life. Such a distinctive ornament served to remind the Israelites that God had established a covenant with them. Such a covenant fellowship between the believers and the Lord is even more intimate in the New Testament. How clearly we ought to keep that privilege in mind, even without tassels to remind us!

As we look to the time of Christ it would seem that Jesus wore tassels. At least that seems to be the implication of the text when the woman quietly came up behind him and touched the edge of his cloak (Matthew 9:20; Luke 8:44). On the other hand, the Pharisees, in a way so typical of their self-righteousness, made much of the size of the tassels they put on their garments (Matthew 23:5). We see again how Satan can take what God intends for good and turn it into a misguided, work-righteous act.

THE YEARS OF WANDERING

Life in the Community

During the forty years of wandering in the wilderness a tragic event illustrates the rebellious mood that affected most of the people of Israel. That event is the rebellion of Korah. It was a clear challenge to the Lord. The people rejected both Moses, their national leader, and Aaron, their High Priest and mediator. The rebellion showed that God was indeed just in letting the disobedient generation die in the wilderness.

The Double Rebellion

16 Korah son of Izhar, the son of Kohath, the son of Levi, and certain Reubenites — Dathan and Abiram, sons of Eliab, and On son of Peleth — became insolent ²and rose up against Moses. With them were 250 Israelite men, well-known community leaders who had been appointed members of the council. ³They came as a group to oppose Moses and Aaron and said to them, "You have gone too far! The whole community is holy, every one of them, and the LORD is with them. Why then do you set yourselves above the LORD's assembly?"

⁴When Moses heard this, he fell facedown. ⁵Then he said to Korah and all his followers: "In the morning the LORD will show who belongs to him and who is holy, and he will have that person come near him. The man he chooses he will cause to come near him. ⁶You, Korah, and all your followers are to do this: Take censers ⁷and tomorrow put fire and incense in them before the LORD. The man the LORD chooses will be the one who is holy. You Levites have gone too far!"

[8]Moses also said to Korah, "Now listen, you Levites! [9]Isn't it enough for you that the God of Israel has separated you from the rest of the Israelite community and brought you near himself to do the work at the LORD's tabernacle and to stand before the community and minister to them? [10]He has brought you and all your fellow Levites near himself, but now you are trying to get the priesthood too. [11]It is against the LORD that you and all your followers have banded together. Who is Aaron that you should grumble against him?"

[12]Then Moses summoned Dathan and Abiram, the sons of Eliab. But they said, "We will not come! [13]Isn't it enough that you have brought us up out of a land flowing with milk and honey to kill us in the desert? And now you also want to lord it over us? [14]Moreover, you haven't brought us into a land flowing with milk and honey or given us an inheritance of fields and vineyards. Will you gouge out the eyes of these men? No, we will not come!"

[15]Then Moses became very angry and said to the LORD, "Do not accept their offering. I have not taken so much as a donkey from them, nor have I wronged any of them."

[16]Moses said to Korah, "You and all your followers are to appear before the LORD tomorrow — you and they and Aaron. [17]Each man is to take his censer and put incense in it — 250 censers in all — and present it before the LORD. You and Aaron are to present your censers also." [18]So each man took his censer, put fire and incense in it, and stood with Moses and Aaron at the entrance to the Tent of Meeting. [19]When Korah had gathered all his followers in opposition to them at the entrance to the Tent of Meeting, the glory of the LORD appeared to the entire assembly. [20]The LORD said to Moses and Aaron, [21]"Separate yourselves from this assembly so I can put an end to them at once."

[22]But Moses and Aaron fell face down and cried out, "O God, God of the spirits of all mankind, will you be angry with the entire assembly when only one man sins?"

The rebellion had had its small beginnings in the grumbling at the edge of the camp. It had grown with the rebellion of Miriam and Aaron. The climax of that rebelliousness had occurred at Kadesh when the people had refused to go forward into the Promised Land.

It was very natural that such attitudes of rebellion should become even more pronounced after the Israelites were turned back from entering Canaan. Unwilling to admit their own guilt, the frustrations of some jelled in the rebellion of Korah. In defiance (see 15:31) they blamed their leaders and God for their unfortunate circumstances. Although this revolution was openly directed at Moses and Aaron, it shows clearly that all sin is really rebellion against God.

This rebellion, just as the incident with the Sabbath-breaker, only shows more clearly that God had acted justly with a rebellious generation. Though some arguments would place this incident late in the thirty-eight year exile in the wilderness, it seems to fit more naturally as an immediate sequel to the incident with the spies.

How natural that thoughts of rebellion would follow from the events at Kadesh-barnea. First, the people refused to go forward under the Lord's blessing. Then they insisted on going forward under their own power, even though the Lord warned them against it. When they were defeated and Moses had not gone with them, what is more natural than to use him and Aaron as scapegoats? What is more natural for sinful human beings than to shift all the blame for their actions on others and especially on their leaders? In paraphrase of Adam's words in Genesis 3:12 we can almost hear them say: "The leaders you put here, Lord, have misguided us. Because of them we failed to enter the Promised Land."

From such attitudes the two-pronged rebellion was spawned. It was directed against the priesthood of Aaron and against the national leadership of Moses. At its head, as the chief spokesman, was Korah who aspired to be promoted from Levite to priest. Korah was in a leadership role because he was a close relative of Aaron and Moses (Exodus 6:18). Full support came from three leaders in the tribe of Reuben. They were apparently unhappy because their tribe was not in a leading role, even though Reuben had been Jacob's oldest son. An even broader base for the rebellion was provided by 250 other leaders of the nation.

The first statement of the rebels revealed the false ideas that were behind their actions (Numbers 16:3). The error does not come through clearly in translation because two key Hebrew words are not clearly distinguished. The one word means the people according to the natural organization, that is, the nation. The other word means the people according to its divine calling and God-given purpose, that is, the church.

The statement of the rebels confused these two words. Instead of saying that the church, the group of faithful believers, was holy, Korah asserted that the entire nation was holy, and for emphasis added the words "every one of them." The absurdity of this statement is self-evident when a person looks back to the ways in which the people had erred since leaving Egypt. Here again the ugly apparition of false national pride reveals itself, as it had when Miriam and Aaron had challenged the leadership of Moses (Numbers 12:1).

The next assertion of the rebels, "And the LORD is in their midst," is in itself a correct statement. It is the truthful part of the rebels' allegations that gave their claim the appearance of correctness. But the self-righteousness that characterized later Judaism is already revealed. The tone indicated that the followers of Korah looked at the presence of God as a right that belonged to them, rather than an evidence of God's love based on a covenant of grace.

135

How quickly they had forgotten the condition attached to their calling: "If you obey me fully and keep my covenant" (Exodus 19:5).

On these false premises the rebels alleged that Moses and Aaron had set themselves up as the leaders of the Israelites. The final allegation of Numbers 16:3 was directed at the offices of Moses and Aaron. The rebels completely overlooked the fact that God himself had chosen Moses and Aaron. He had appointed them. He had designated them as mediators between himself and the congregation. He had instructed them to train this people to fulfill their God-given function of some day bringing forth the Savior of all mankind.

The rebels' challenge was now in the open. They claimed that Moses and Aaron were arrogant usurpers. As such, they did not deserve the offices of spiritual and national leadership in Israel.

Moses' first reaction was to fall to his face in the Tent of Meeting (Numbers 16:5). He may have wondered why the Lord had not struck down Korah and his followers on the spot. Moses sensed the blasphemy in their false assertions about the holiness of Israel. But the Lord chose to wait until the next day. At his chosen time the Lord himself would make it very clear that he had called Moses and Aaron to their positions of leadership.

The proposed procedure was simple and direct. The test would be based on the Lord's command that only priests were to burn incense in the tabernacle. If Korah and his followers brought their censers and burned incense in the tabernacle, their defiance of God's ordinances would be unmistakably evident. Therefore the chosen procedure would give God the opportunity to show whether he would accept the incense offerings of Korah and his followers instead of the incense offering of Aaron, the high priest.

But even as Moses outlined the procedure, he felt compelled to warn Korah and his followers to consider carefully what they were doing. "You have gone too far" (Numbers 16:7). Wasn't it privilege enough that they had been separated for the service of the tabernacle as Levites? "Are you seeking for the priesthood also?" Then Moses also pointed out the ultimate seriousness of their challenge by saying, "You and all your company are gathered together against the Lord; but as for Aaron, who is he that you grumble against him?" (Numbers 16:11) In this statement Moses put his finger on the real issue that was before them — their rebellion was against the Lord, who had designated and called Aaron as high priest.

The Judgment of the Lord

²³Then the LORD said to Moses, ²⁴"Say to the assembly, 'Move away from the tents of Korah, Dathan and Abiram!'"

²⁵Moses got up and went to Dathan and Abiram, and the elders of Israel followed him. ²⁶He warned the assembly, "Move back from the tents of these wicked men! Do not touch anything belonging to them, or you will be swept away because of all their sins." ²⁷So they moved away from the tents of Korah, Dathan and Abiram. Dathan and Abiram had come out and were standing with their wives, children and little ones at the entrances to their tents.

²⁸Then Moses said, "This is how you will know that the LORD has sent me to do all these things and that it was not my idea: ²⁹If these men die a natural death and experience only what usually happens to men, then the LORD has not sent me. ³⁰But if the LORD brings about something totally new, and the earth opens its mouth and swallows them, with everything that belongs to them, and they go down alive into the grave, then you will know that these men have treated the LORD with contempt."

³¹As soon as he finished saying all this, the ground under them split apart ³²and the earth opened its mouth and swallowed them, with their households and all Korah's men and all their

possessions. [33] They went down alive into the grave, with everything they owned; the earth closed over them, and they perished and were gone from the community. [34] At their cries, all the Israelites around them fled, shouting, "The earth is going to swallow us too!"

[35] And fire came out from the LORD and consumed the 250 men who were offering the incense.

[36] The LORD said to Moses, [37] "Tell Eleazar son of Aaron, the priest, to take the censers out of the smoldering remains and scatter the coals some distance away, for the censers are holy — [38] the censers of the men who sinned at the cost of their lives. Hammer the censers into sheets to overlay the altar, for they were presented before the LORD and have become holy. Let them be a sign to the Israelites."

[39] So Eleazar the priest collected the bronze censers brought by those who had been burned up, and he had them hammered out to overlay the altar, [40] as the LORD directed him through Moses. This was to remind the Israelites that no one except a descendant of Aaron should come to burn incense before the LORD, or he would become like Korah and his followers.

The second challenge was directed against Moses' leadership. In order to bring the matter into the open Moses summoned Dathan and Abiram, the primary co-conspirators (Numbers 16:12ff). Insolently those leaders refused to obey the summons. The complaint against Moses was that he had led the people into the wilderness to die. By describing Egypt as a land of milk and honey, they were ignoring the years of slavery and suffering that the people had endured. Further, they complained that Moses' method of administration was a mere "lording it over us" (Numbers 16:13). Still further, he had failed to carry out his promise to bring them to a land flowing with milk and honey. Really it was all Moses' fault that the people had been deprived of their inheritance. Enough was enough! Moses would not be allowed to throw dust in their eyes any more. "We will not come up!" (Numbers 16:14).

When this report was brought to Moses, his patience ran out. In no way had he been a heartless taskmaster to the people. He had not even taken a donkey from them. "I have done no harm to anyone." Yet Moses set the problem before the Lord, even while he asserted that the whole accusation was groundless.

Though Moses seemed to want an immediate solution, the Lord chose to wait for the final settlement of this rebellion till the following day.

So Moses repeated the directions for Korah and his followers, reminding them to appear on the next day with their censers, and assuring them, that Aaron would do likewise.

The next day dawned. Korah and his company dared to show up at the tabernacle. With no fear they stepped right up to the doorway of the Tent of Meeting, the place where the priests were to function. In moral support of Korah's claim, the people had assembled outside. The influence of the rebellion had already spread far.

But the time for God's judgment had come. The "Glory of the LORD," that is, the light by which God manifested his presence among the Israelites, appeared (Numbers 16:19). As Moses had indicated, the real issue was that the Lord's arrangements were being challenged by the rebels. Therefore the Lord decided the issue. Because the people had supplied moral support to Korah and the other rebels, God was again ready to consume the entire nation "instantly" (Numbers 16:21).

In this crisis Moses and Aaron still pleaded with the Lord on behalf of the people. Moses, as the spokesman, appealed to God as the author of life, and presented the argument that, even though one person sins, God should not be angry with the entire nation. In mercy the Lord relented regarding the whole people.

But the rebels had to be punished! Immediately! God instructed Moses to urge the people to move away from the tents of Dathan, Abiram and the other leaders. But even this warning did not reach the hearts of the ringleaders.

Then Moses moved toward the tents of Dathan and Abiram. He made the additional announcement that if the rebels would die a natural death, it would be proper to conclude that the Lord had not chosen him. But they weren't going to die a natural death. The ground would open up and swallow the rebels.

But the rebels were still unmoved. In an attitude of challenge, Dathan and Abiram stood at the doors of their tents with their families. They watched defiantly as Moses approached.

Moses had hardly finished speaking when the terrifying punishment occurred. The ground opened and swallowed Korah, Dathan and Abiram, their households, their followers and all their possessions. They were literally wiped off the face of the earth without a trace.

The sudden and overwhelming catastrophe made the people draw back in panic. They feared lest the catastrophe envelop them also.

Meanwhile back at the tabernacle the Lord acted in judgment on the 250 men who were offering incense. Flames shot out from the "glory of the LORD." In a manner similar to the way God punished Nadab and Abihu (see Leviticus 10), who had also come into the tabernacle with strange fire, the 250 men who were offering incense at the tabernacle were consumed with fire. The devastation seems to have been more complete in this situation, however, since there is no mention of burying these people (Numbers 16:35). Apparently the fire from the Lord consumed them completely. The 250 men had vanished. The only remnants were the censers that they had used. Since these bronze incense-burners had been presented in the tabernacle, the Lord considered them consecrated to himself. Therefore Eleazar was instructed to gather the censers and hammer them into a bronze covering for the altar. In the years to come this covering on the great altar was a constant reminder "that no layman who is not of the descendants of Aaron should come near to burn incense before the LORD."

A special note needs to be added about the sons of Korah who appear on other pages of the Scripture. Apparently not all of Korah's sons joined in his rebellion. Consequently, they did not die. The descendants are mentioned as singers in connection with some Psalms. An example is Psalm 42. Although God does punish generation after generation of unfaithful people, it is just as clear that he will remember and bless those who are faithful to him. He can find a way to use them in his service.

A Mediator Needed Again

⁴¹The next day the whole Israelite community grumbled against Moses and Aaron "You have killed the LORD's people," they said.

⁴²But when the assembly gathered in opposition to Moses and Aaron and turned toward the Tent of Meeting, suddenly the cloud covered it and the glory of the LORD appeared. ⁴³Then Moses and Aaron went to the front of the Tent of Meeting, ⁴⁴and the LORD said to Moses, ⁴⁵"Get away from this assembly so I can put an end to them at once." And they fell facedown.

⁴⁶Then Moses said to Aaron, "Take your censer and put incense in it, along with fire from the altar, and hurry to the assembly to make atonement for them. Wrath has come out from the LORD; the plague has started." ⁴⁷So Aaron did as Moses said, and ran into the midst of the assembly. The plague had already started among the people, but Aaron offered the incense and made

atonement for them. ⁴⁸He stood between the living and the dead, and the plague stopped. ⁴⁹But 14,700 people died from the plague, in addition to those who had died because of Korah. ⁵⁰Then Aaron returned to Moses at the entrance to the Tent of Meeting, for the plague had stopped.

The need to find a scapegoat still reared its ugly head among the people! They were awed by the events that destroyed Korah and his followers. Sad to say, however, these judgments of God did not lead them to repentance. On the very next day all the people once again gathered in rebellion against Moses and Aaron. "You are the ones who caused the death of the LORD's people," they said (Numbers 16:41). What an exalted view they had of Korah and his followers! What a superstitious view they had of the powers of Moses and Aaron! The Lord's judgment on Korah had clearly shown God's stamp of approval on Moses and Aaron. But the people accused them of selfishly and magically retaining their offices by wiping out the "true people of God."

Whether in hope of relief or in anticipation of further punishment, Moses and Aaron instinctively turned toward the Tent of Meeting. They were not disappointed. The "glory of the LORD" appeared again. Again the Lord was ready to consume the entire people in an instant.

What should Moses now say? He had pleaded eloquently at Mount Sinai. He had also pleaded faithfully at Kadesh-barnea. The previous day he had groped desperately to find an argument to keep the Lord from wiping out the nation. What could be said in behalf of a people that was again rebelling? Moses rose to the occasion. He used God's own arrangement — the incense offering — offered by God's designated high priest, Aaron. Moses instructed Aaron to make an incense offering immediately, since a plague had already started among the people.

Aaron obeyed. With the boldness proper for God's appointed servant Aaron moved out among the people to stand between the living and the dead. The courage to go out among the people who moments before had been so surly is certainly to be noted and commended. He functioned as high priest for the people even in their sinfulness. His example is worthy of imitation by all who are called to be public ministers of the gospel.

Through Aaron's action the plague was checked.

But the Lord's severity was still evident; 14,700 died of the plague, "in addition to those who had died because of Korah" (16:49). Yet the goodness of the Lord is also evident. He did preserve this people and he kept his promises to them. According to his gracious purposes he sustained them during the remaining years in the wilderness.

How graciously the Lord had also provided for his people through the priesthood. Aaron clearly demonstrated the substitutionary and mediatorial work of the priest. He was ready to offer himself between life and death. The incense he offered represented prayer before the Lord. When Moses had run out of words and reasons, the prayers implied in the incense offering were enough to hold off God's wrath. How well we might remember the function of the Holy Spirit in which he "intercedes for us with groans that words cannot express" (Romans 8:26). Surely that work of the Holy Spirit was functioning when the Lord stopped the plague.

THE YEARS OF WANDERING

Life in Worship

The previous day God had demonstrated the importance of Aaron's priesthood by a startling act of judgment. God now chose a beautiful symbol to give additional proof that he had chosen Aaron as the High Priest. He demonstrated this in the miracle of the budding staff. Another aspect of the Lord's will involved additional guidelines for the priests and Levites. For the worship life of his Old Testament people the Lord chose to define exactly how the water of cleansing was to be prepared. It was to be used in the purification of those who were ceremonially unclean.

The Budding of Aaron's Staff

17 The LORD said to Moses, [2]"Speak to the Israelites and get twelve staffs from them, one from the leader of each of their ancestral tribes. Write the name of each man on his staff. [3]On the staff of Levi write Aaron's name, for there must be one staff for the head of each ancestral tribe. [4]Place them in the Tent of Meeting in front of the Testimony, where I meet with you. [5]The staff belonging to the man I choose will sprout, and I will rid myself of this constant grumbling against you by the Israelites."

[6]So Moses spoke to the Israelites, and their leaders gave him twelve staffs, one for the leader of each of their ancestral tribes, and Aaron's staff was among them. [7]Moses placed the staffs before the LORD in the Tent of the Testimony.

[8]The next day Moses entered the Tent of the Testimony and saw that Aaron's staff, which represented the house of Levi, had not only sprouted but had budded, blossomed and produced

almonds. ⁹Then Moses brought out all the staffs from the Lord's presence to all the Israelites. They looked at them, and each man took his own staff.

¹⁰The Lord said to Moses, "Put back Aaron's staff in front of the Testimony, to be kept as a sign to the rebellious. This will put an end to their grumbling against me, so that they will not die." ¹¹Moses did just as the Lord commanded him.

¹²The Israelites said to Moses, "We will die! We are lost, we are all lost! ¹³Anyone who even comes near the tabernacle of the Lord will die. Are we all going to die?"

The Lord chose to act in another way to squelch the rebellion. His goal was to rid himself of the constant grumbling against him by the Israelites. Therefore the Lord chose a sign, by which the people would know that Aaron was indeed the one whom he had chosen to be the high priest. The test was simple enough! The leader of each of the tribes was to bring a staff. To avoid any uncertainty, each leader's name was to be written on his staff. For this particular test Aaron was to bring the staff for the Levites.

The Lord promised that the staff of the man he had chosen would sprout. So the staffs were placed in the innermost part of the Tabernacle overnight. The dead wood of one staff would again become alive and would show that life by sprouting. With his usual meticulous care Moses followed the Lord's directions.

The next day the staffs were brought out, and the amazing power and the special selection of the Lord became evident to all. For Aaron's staff had not only sprouted leaves, it had also budded, blossomed and produced almonds. Not only had the Lord given the dead staff life but what normally takes weeks and months had occurred overnight. By contrast, none of the other staffs had produced anything. They were dead and barren. The Lord's sign clearly undergirded the priesthood of Aaron.

The Lord had a further purpose for Aaron's staff. He wanted it to be kept in the tabernacle. The staff would serve as a sign to succeeding generations that the Lord had chosen only Aaron and his descendants for the priesthood and high priesthood.

Even putting the staff in the tabernacle was an act of mercy. The Lord hoped to get rid of the grumbling against him. Whether the grumblers realized it or not, criticizing the leaders whom the Lord had chosen was equivalent to criticizing the Lord himself. Therefore the Lord wanted the grumbling to cease. He did not want his own patience to run out. He wanted them to have clear evidence "so that they will not die" (Numbers 17:10). On the other hand, the signs were clear. There would be no excuse for the people if they turned their backs on him and were destroyed.

The Lord had done exactly what he had promised. But the people overreacted once more. Note the ascending order of their words: "die — lost — all lost — even come near the tabernacle — all going to die?" In the psychology of crowds they proceeded from what was true, overlaid it with emotion and reached a gross exaggeration. Again and again Satan cleverly uses this psychological error to make the Lord seem so unreasonable! How wonderful that God does not act according to the excesses of man! What a merciful and gracious Lord we have! He even forgives such human foibles and exaggerations!

In conclusion it should be noted that the rod of Aaron is intended by God as a picture of the eternal priesthood of Christ, who is able to save those who come to God by him, seeing he ever lives to make intercession for them (Hebrews 7:24,25).

146

Duties of Priests and Levites

18 The LORD said to Aaron, "You, your sons and your father's family are to bear the responsibility for offenses against the sanctuary, and you and your sons alone are to bear the responsibility for offenses against the priesthood. ²Bring your fellow Levites from your ancestral tribe to join you and assist you when you and your sons minister before the Tent of Testimony. ³They are to be responsible to you and are to perform all the duties of the Tent, but they must not go near the furnishings of the sanctuary or the altar, or both they and you will die. ⁴They are to join you and be responsible for the care of the Tent of Meeting — all the work at the Tent — and no one else may come near where you are.

⁵"You are to be responsible for the care of the sanctuary and the altar, so that wrath will not fall on the Israelites again. ⁶I myself have selected your fellow Levites from among the Israelites as a gift to you, dedicated to the LORD to do the work at the Tent of Meeting. ⁷But only you and your sons may serve as priests in connection with everything at the altar and inside the curtain. I am giving you the service of the priesthood as a gift. Anyone else who comes near the sanctuary must be put to death."

Had the Levites forfeited their position by the rebellion of Korah? To answer any questions like that, the Lord now addressed Aaron directly and thus chose to make it clear that the Levites were still to serve in the tabernacle. Aaron (the high priest) and his sons (the priests) and his father's family were to bear the responsibility for any offenses against the sanctuary. Only the high priest and the priests would bear the responsibility for any sins against the priesthood, that is, against the proper functioning of the priests. What a solemn responsibility! Nothing was to be done to bring shame on either the tabernacle or the priesthood.

Previous instructions had focused on the moving and care of the tabernacle. This section focuses on the service that the

Levites were to provide in support of the priests in their priestly functions. Clearly it was the intention of the Lord that the faithful Levites were to serve after the rebellion of Korah.

The work of the Levites dealt especially with external parts of the tabernacle. The limits were very clear. Since the tabernacle was indeed the place where the Lord's glory dwelt on earth, only the priests were allowed to deal with the furnishings of the sanctuary or the altar. So the Levites were made responsible to the priests and the priests were responsible to God. If either the priests or the Levites failed to follow the Lord's commands, they would forfeit their lives.

The Lord again underscores these directions by emphasizing that he does not want destruction to fall on the Israelites. So the care of the sanctuary and the altar was to be assigned to the priests alone. In these matters the Levites were not permitted to substitute for the priests.

To head off the temptation to presumption like Korah's, the Lord described the service of the priesthood as a "gift" (18:7). Neither the office of the priest nor the privilege of serving as a Levite was earned. In grace the Lord had given the priesthood to the family of Aaron. In another act of loving-kindness the Levites were provided to assist the priests. Therefore both the priests and the Levites were most appropriately described as God's gifts to Israel. Indeed, the honor of serving within the tabernacle is also called a gift. Neither the Levites nor the descendants of Aaron had the right to demand this honor or responsibility from God. It was assigned to them as a gracious act of God. They would have the high honor of serving God directly and at the same time serving as a gift to the people. What a privilege to be leaders in worshipping the gracious and merciful God!

148

In the New Testament the Lord has not set aside such a group of people who are to serve in a priesthood as man's go-betweens with God. Indeed the Bible directly calls all believers kings and priests in the kingdom of God (Revelation 1:6). What an honor the Lord bestows on each believer that he should be a priest who can approach God directly and address him as "Our Father!" What a special gift we should consider this relationship! How gladly we ought serve so generous a God, for we also receive our privileges only as a gift of God's grace! Yet the Lord also says that those who are called to be leaders in the church are gifts (Ephesians 4:11).

Offerings for Priests and Levites

8Then the LORD said to Aaron, "I myself have put you in charge of the offerings presented to me; all the holy offerings the Israelites give me I give to you and your sons as your portion and regular share. 9You are to have the part of the most holy offerings that is kept from the fire. From all the gifts they bring me as most holy offerings, whether grain or sin or guilt offerings, that part belongs to you and your sons. 10Eat it as something most holy; every male shall eat it. You must regard it as holy.

11"This also is yours: whatever is set aside from the gifts of all the wave offerings of the Israelites. I give this to you and your sons and daughters as your regular share. Everyone in your household who is ceremonially clean may eat it.

12"I give you all the finest olive oil and all the finest new wine and grain they give the LORD as the firstfruits of their harvest. 13All the land's firstfruits that they bring to the LORD will be yours. Everyone in your household who is ceremonially clean may eat it.

14"Everything in Israel that is devoted to the LORD is yours. 15The first offspring of every womb, both man and animal, that is offered to the LORD is yours. But you must redeem every firstborn son and every firstborn male of unclean animals. 16When they are

a month old, you must redeem them at the redemption price set at five shekels of silver, according to the sanctuary shekel, which weighs twenty gerahs. ¹⁷"But you must not redeem the firstborn of an ox, a sheep or a goat; they are holy. Sprinkle their blood on the altar and burn their fat as an offering made by fire, an aroma pleasing to the LORD. ¹⁸Their meat is to be yours, just as the breast of the wave offering and the right thigh are yours. ¹⁹Whatever is set aside from the holy offerings the Israelites present to the LORD I give to you and your sons and daughters as your regular share. It is an everlasting covenant of salt before the LORD for both you and your offspring."

²⁰The LORD said to Aaron, "You will have no inheritance in their land, nor will you have any share among them; I am your share and your inheritance among the Israelites.

²¹"I give to the Levites all the tithes in Israel as their inheritance in return for the work they do while serving at the Tent of Meeting. ²²From now on the Israelites must not go near the Tent of Meeting, or they will bear the consequences of their sin and will die. ²³It is the Levites who are to do the work at the Tent of Meeting and bear the responsibility for offenses against it. This is a lasting ordinance for the generations to come. They will receive no inheritance among the Israelites. ²⁴Instead, I give to the Levites as their inheritance the tithes that the Israelites present as an offering to the LORD. That is why I said concerning them: 'They will have no inheritance among the Israelites.' "

²⁵The LORD said to Moses, ²⁶"Speak to the Levites and say to them: 'When you receive from the Israelites the tithe I give you as your inheritance, you must present a tenth of that tithe as the LORD's offering. ²⁷Your offering will be reckoned to you as grain from the threshing floor or juice from the winepress. ²⁸In this way you also will present an offering to the LORD from all the tithes you receive from the Israelites. From these tithes you must give the LORD's portion to Aaron the priest. ²⁹You must present as the LORD's portion the best and holiest part of everything given to you.'

³⁰"Say to the Levites: 'When you present the best part, it will be reckoned to you as the product of the threshing floor or the winepress. ³¹You and your households may eat the rest of it anywhere, for it is your wages for your work at the Tent of Meeting. ³²By presenting the best part of it you will not be guilty in this matter; then you will not defile the holy offerings of the Israelites, and you will not die.' "

The key word in the heading of this section is the word "for." Instead of considering the offerings that were made by the priests, the Lord tells us how the offerings were also to serve as support for the priests and Levites. In this section the Lord indicates that certain parts of the offerings that were not consumed by fire were to be given to the priests and Levites.

The priests were to have those portions of the grain offerings, sin offerings, and guilt offerings that were not consumed by the fire on the Lord's altar. Of these offerings every male in the priest's family could eat. Their whole behavior was to show that the offering was something that was truly holy, or committed to the Lord.

From the wave offerings, the offering of firstfruits and other offerings that were consigned to the Lord, everyone in the priests' households could eat. The only limitation within the priest's family was that each person should be ceremonially clean.

Giving these portions of the offerings to the priests was the Lord's way of giving them an inheritance among the Israelites. Because the priests devoted their lives to the work in the tabernacle, the Lord provided for them through the offerings rather than through an inheritance of land.

In a similar way the Lord provided for the Levites, whose lives were also to be dedicated to the service of the tabernacle. The Levites received the tithes that the people brought to the Lord. Through this arrangement the Lord

151

was providing an inheritance for the Levites. They were thus able to devote themselves fully to the work of the Lord. Like the priests the Levites did not receive an inheritance of land. Their inheritance would be in their work at the Lord's house.

According to these instructions the Levites were to give to the priests one tenth of the offerings that they received. The priests in turn were to give a tenth of what they received to the high priest. The principle that even those who serve the Lord directly in the church are to bring offerings is clearly presented. But just as surely this whole section presents the principle that the laborer is worthy of his hire. The people who devote themselves to the fulltime work of the Lord are entitled to receive their living from that work. The same principle is applied in both Testaments.

The Waters of Cleansing

19 The LORD said to Moses and Aaron: ²"This is a requirement of the law that the LORD has commanded: Tell the Israelites to bring you a red heifer without defect or blemish and that has never been under a yoke. ³Give it to Eleazar the priest; it is to be taken outside the camp and slaughtered in his presence. ⁴Then Eleazar the priest is to take some of its blood on his finger and sprinkle it seven times toward the front of the Tent of Meeting. ⁵While he watches, the heifer is to be burned — its hide, flesh, blood and offal. ⁶The priest is to take some cedar wood, hyssop and scarlet wool and throw them onto the burning heifer. ⁷After that, the priest must wash his clothes and bathe himself with water. He may then come into the camp, but he will be ceremonially unclean till evening. ⁸The man who burns it must also wash his clothes and bathe with water, and he too will be unclean till evening.

⁹"A man who is clean shall gather up the ashes of the heifer and put them in a ceremonially clean place outside the camp. They shall be kept by the Israelite community for use in the water of cleansing; it is for purification from sin. ¹⁰The man who gathers

up the ashes of the heifer must also wash his clothes, and he too will be unclean till evening. This will be a lasting ordinance both for the Israelites and for the aliens living among them.

11"Whoever touches the dead body of anyone will be unclean for seven days. 12He must purify himself with the water on the third day and on the seventh day; then he will be clean. But if he does not purify himself on the third and seventh days, he will not be clean. 13Whoever touches the dead body of anyone and fails to purify himself defiles the LORD's tabernacle. That person must be cut off from Israel. Because the water of cleansing has not been sprinkled on him, he is unclean; his uncleanness remains on him.

14"This is the law that applies when a person dies in a tent: Anyone who enters the tent and anyone who is in it will be unclean for seven days, 15and every open container without a lid fastened on it will be unclean.

16"Anyone out in the open who touches someone who has been killed with a sword or someone who has died a natural death, or anyone who touches a human bone or a grave, will be unclean for seven days.

17"For the unclean person, put some ashes from the burned purification offering into a jar and pour fresh water over them. 18Then a man who is ceremonially clean is to take some hyssop, dip it in the water and sprinkle the tent and all the furnishings and the people who were there. He must also sprinkle anyone who has touched a human bone or a grave or someone who has been killed or someone who has died a natural death. 19The man who is clean is to sprinkle the unclean person on the third and seventh days, and on the seventh day he is to purify him. The person being cleansed must wash his clothes and bathe with water, and that evening he will be clean. 20But if a person who is unclean does not purify himself, he must be cut off from the community, because he has defiled the sanctuary of the LORD. The water of cleansing has not been sprinkled on him, and he is unclean. 21This is a lasting ordinance for them.

"The man who sprinkles the water of cleansing must also wash his clothes, and anyone who touches the water of cleansing will

be unclean till evening. ²²Anything that an unclean person touches becomes unclean, and anyone who touches it becomes unclean till evening."

A whole generation of Israel was to die in the wilderness. The slow countdown of death was in progress. Against such a background the Lord now gave instructions both about the ceremonial uncleanness that occurred in connection with death and about the purification from that uncleanness.

In the Garden of Eden death had entered the world as a punishment for sin. In God's view, therefore death was "unclean." Death was an intrusion into God's perfect world. An Israelite who even touched a dead person was ceremonially unclean. For seven days the unclean person was excluded from the religious life of the people. That person was also socially isolated, since anyone who came in contact with him would become unclean. On the third and seventh day certain rituals had to be followed in order to restore the person to the state of cleanness.

In order to carry out the cleansing ritual a certain type of ashes had to be prepared. A red heifer was to be burned in its entirety, including its blood, outside of the camp. The ashes were to be increased by adding cedar wood, hyssop and scarlet wool. The resulting ashes were available to be used in the water of cleansing which was used in the purification ritual for the ceremonially unclean.

Verses 11-16 define the situations in which a person became ceremonially unclean in connection with a dead body. The basic principle was that anyone who touched a dead body, or even touched a bone or a grave of a human being, was to be unclean for seven days. The status of uncleanness would also extend to open materials and containers which had been within a tent where someone died.

Among the factors that made the uncleanness so difficult was the fact that anything the person touched would also become unclean.

Beginning with verse 17, the chapter focuses on the ritual of purification. A vital part of this ritual was the water of purification in which the ashes of a red heifer had been placed. On the third and seventh day the water of purification had to be sprinkled over the person and over everything that had become unclean through contact with a dead body. On the seventh day the person who had been unclean also had to wash his clothes and bathe as part of the purification process.

There were additional spinoffs of uncleanness. The person who sprinkled the water of cleansing also became unclean till evening.

This chapter helps us understand some events in the New Testament. For example, the desire of the Jewish leaders to have Jesus and the two malefactors removed from the crosses by sundown is based on the fact that death would produce uncleanness on a holy day. They urged Pilate to order that the bones of the crucified people should be broken, in order to hasten death.

Furthermore, to warn a person who might accidentally make himself unclean, all burial areas and sepulchres were whitewashed. The custom provides background for Jesus' statement that the Pharisees were "whitewashed sepulchres" (Matthew 23:27). The symbolism of Christ's statement was that his opponents were really spiritually dead and anybody who associated with them would also become unclean in God's sight and die.

The ceremonial uncleanness that surrounded the dead person led to the custom of quick burial among the Jews. At the time of Christ Jews regularly buried their dead within twenty-four hours.

155

How different the situation is in the New Testament era as we hear the glorious news that through the death and resurrection of Christ death is swallowed up in victory for believers. Because of our victory in Christ, death no longer defeats or defiles us. Instead, in Christ, death becomes the gateway to heaven. Therefore death is now a victory by which we enter into the presence of the Lord through all eternity.

There is another carry-over of this particular part of the Old Testament ritual. Hebrews 9:13,14 refers to the ashes of the heifer, stating: "The blood of goats and bulls and the ashes of a heifer sprinkled on those who are ceremonially unclean sanctify them so that they are outwardly clean. How much more, then, will the blood of Christ, who through the eternal Spirit offered himself unblemished to God, cleanse our consciences from acts that lead to death, so that we may serve the living God?" Hebrews 10:19-22 draws a parallel between the sprinkling and our cleansing in the blood of Christ: "Therefore, brothers, since we have confidence to enter the Most Holy Place by the blood of Jesus, by a new and living way opened for us through the curtain, that is, his body, and since we have a great priest over the house of God, let us draw near to God with a sincere heart in full assurance of faith, having our hearts sprinkled to cleanse us from a guilty conscience and having our bodies washed with pure water."

PART III
FROM KADESH TO THE JORDAN

NUMBERS 20—27

The forty years of wandering in the wilderness were almost at an end. The children of Israel gathered once again at Kadesh. At long last the Lord was about to carry out his promise to the people.

The third part of the book of Numbers covers a rather short span of time. The Israelites now moved forward rather speedily from Kadesh in the south to the eastern banks of the Jordan River. There are some more examples of complaining and of problems. There are also remarkable examples of the Lord's care before hostile armies and before a greedy prophet. How clearly the people could have exclaimed, "The Lord is with us! He cares for us while moving out, in a life in the community and as individuals."

Life While Moving Out

When so large a group of people gathered at Kadesh the second time, a familiar problem arose. There was not enough water. When the people started to complain, it almost seemed that they would again be denied entrance into the Promised Land. But the Lord provided for them and then led them around the land of Edom, along the edge of the Arabian desert. The events surrounding the bronze snake reminded the Israelites of God's goodness. The events surrounding the defeat of King Sihon and King Og demonstrated God's power. So under God's protection his people finally encamped at the Jordan River.

Water from the Rock

20 In the first month the whole Israelite community arrived at the Desert of Zin, and they stayed at Kadesh. There Miriam died and was buried.

²Now there was no water for the community, and the people gathered in opposition to Moses and Aaron. ³They quarreled with Moses and said, "If only we had died when our brothers fell dead before the LORD! ⁴Why did you bring the LORD's community into this desert, that we and our livestock should die here? ⁵Why did you bring us up out of Egypt to this terrible place? It has no grain or figs, grapevines or pomegranates. And there is no water to drink!"

⁶Moses and Aaron went from the assembly to the entrance to the Tent of Meeting and fell facedown, and the glory of the LORD appeared to them. ⁷The LORD said to Moses, ⁸"Take the staff, and you and your brother Aaron gather the assembly together. Speak to that rock before their eyes and it will pour out its water. You will bring water out of the rock for the community so they and their livestock can drink."

⁹So Moses took the staff from the LORD's presence, just as he commanded him. ¹⁰He and Aaron gathered the assembly together in front of the rock and Moses said to them, "Listen, you rebels, must we bring you water out of this rock?" ¹¹Then Moses raised his arm and struck the rock twice with his staff. Water gushed out, and the community and their livestock drank.

¹²But the LORD said to Moses and Aaron, "Because you did not trust in me enough to honor me as holy in the sight of the Israelites, you will not bring this community into the land I give them."

¹³These were the waters of Meribah, where the Israelites quarreled with the LORD and where he showed himself holy among them.

The time of exile in the wilderness had come to an end. It is clear from Numbers 20:29 and 33:38 that the first month referred to here is the first month of the fortieth year. From the very spot where the previous journey had been broken off, the people were to set out anew. If the old was interrupted, it had been by the people's unbelief, not by God's failure to keep his promise. Now he resumed his work where it had been interrupted. A little later another census would show that not one of the people who was twenty years old or older when Israel came through the Red Sea was still alive. It was time for the Lord to show that he could indeed bring victory and safety. The very children for whom the parents had predicted destruction thirty-eight years earlier were about to take possession of the Promised Land.

The people again gathered at Kadesh. A single sentence notes that Miriam, Moses' sister died and was buried. Another of the weary and worn pilgrims was home at last.

The ways of sinful man have not changed much over the years. Moses faces a familiar problem. The people didn't have water or their favorite foods. Instead of praying to the Lord for deliverance, they imitated their parents and began to complain against the Lord. They wished for death rather than admitting that they were the problem. They blamed Moses for misleading them. They thought nostalgically of Egypt even though only the oldest ones had been mere children at that time of deliverance. Slavery was not very vivid to them.

Upon hearing these complaints Moses and Aaron followed a familiar procedure. They hurried to the Tent of Meeting. They were frightened by the renewed rebelliousness of the children of Israel. In supplication they fell face-down before the Lord.

159

Once again the Lord manifested his presence by exhibiting his glory. In mercy God chose to give this generation a demonstration of his power. Since this generation had not been adults to witness previous miracles, the Lord chose to act in grace and kindness. His instructions to Moses promised not judgment, but a miracle of mercy. So Moses, functioning with his brother Aaron, was to take his staff; he was to speak to the rock. The rock would provide enough water for the people and their cattle.

For a moment think of all the times Moses reported in tedious detail that he and the people had obeyed the exact word of the Lord. This incident stands in sharp contrast with those situations because here Moses and Aaron disobeyed the Lord. Several things catch our attention as we read the account: "You rebels"; "must *we* bring water"; "struck the rock twice with his staff." The mood expressed by the word "rebels" is far different from the previous attitude of Moses, the mediator, when he prayed for the children of Israel after the idolatry of the golden calf. Another distortion occurs as Moses suggests that he and Aaron are bringing the water from the rock. They were taking glory away from God. Further, the double striking of the rock does not show strict obedience to the command of the Lord. Moses had been instructed to speak to the rock.

In these various ways Moses had failed to follow the instructions of the Lord carefully. Consequently, we see the Lord acting in two directions. It had been his gracious intention all along to provide water for the Israelites. That gift he did provide. But then he addressed Moses and Aaron and told them that he would not permit them to enter the land of Canaan. They had failed to give God the honor due him (Psalm 106:32,33). In effect they had sinned against the First Commandment and therefore God chose

160

to chastise them by withdrawing the blessing of entering the Promised Land.

How clearly this incident shows that the heroes of faith, as admirable as they were on many occasions, were also sinners. The Old Testament heroes also had to trust in the coming Savior for forgiveness of their sins, just as you and I do. Even Moses, who typifies Christ in many of his activities, and Aaron, whose office of high priest prefigured Christ's redemptive work, were both sinners. The Lord considered it wise that they face the chastisement for their sin here on earth. Therefore the Lord withheld from them the privilege of entering the earthly Canaan. On the other hand, since they were both believers we have every reason to believe that they entered the heavenly Canaan, which is a blessing by far greater and more important.

Edom Denies Israel Passage

[14]Moses sent messengers from Kadesh to the king of Edom, saying:

"This is what your brother Israel says: You know about all the hardships that have come upon us. [15]Our forefathers went down into Egypt, and we lived there many years. The Egyptians mistreated us and our fathers, [16]but when we cried out to the LORD, he heard our cry and sent an angel and brought us out of Egypt.

"Now we are here at Kadesh, a town on the edge of your territory. [17]Please let us pass through your country. We will not go through any field or vineyard, or drink water from any well. We will travel along the king's highway and not turn to the right or to the left until we have passed through your territory."

[18]But Edom answered:

"You may not pass through here; if you try, we will march out and attack you with the sword."

161

¹⁹**The Israelites replied:**

"We will go along the main road, and if we or our livestock drink any of your water, we will pay for it. We only want to pass through on foot — nothing else."

²⁰**Again they answered:**

"You may not pass through."

Then Edom came out against them with a large and powerful army. ²¹Since Edom refused to let them go through their territory, Israel turned away from them.

When the children of Israel were in Kadesh, the most direct route to Canaan was through the area inhabited by the Edomites. The Edomites were also descendants of Abraham through his grandson Esau. The initial request for passage drew on this historical fact and identified the Israelites as "your brother Israel" (20:14). The full appeal was based on family relationship, on history, on hardship and on the deliverance by the angel of the Lord.

In spite of the promises of due care and no harm, the request was denied by the king of Edom. Request number two brought refusal number two. To show how serious he was, the king of the Edomites mustered his army in order to meet the Israelites head on.

So under the Lord's guidance the Israelites moved off in a different direction. Since the Edomites were not one of the Canaanite tribes, they were not under the condemnation of the Lord. Therefore Israel did not attack them, and under the Lord's direction they marched southward and eastward in order to move around the land of the Edomites (see map). This meant traveling through the deep depression known as the Arabah, an intensely hot and desolate region, a fact which added to the people's discouragement.

The Death of Aaron

[22]The whole Israelite community set out from Kadesh and came to Mount Hor. [23]At Mount Hor, near the border of Edom, the LORD said to Moses and Aaron, [24]"Aaron will be gathered to his people. He will not enter the land I give the Israelites, because both of you rebelled against my command at the waters of Meribah. [25]Get Aaron and his son Eleazar and take them up Mount Hor. [26]Remove Aaron's garments and put them on his son Eleazar, for Aaron will be gathered to his people; he will die there."

[27]Moses did as the LORD commanded: They went up Mount Hor in the sight of the whole community. [28]Moses removed Aaron's garments and put them on his son Eleazar. And Aaron died there on top of the mountain. Then Moses and Eleazar came down from the mountain, [29]and when the whole community learned that Aaron had died, the entire house of Israel mourned for him thirty days.

Another weary, foot-sore pilgrim was about to die. The Lord chose to summon home to heaven a servant who had served long and well. That person was Aaron. Yet the announcement is presented by the Lord in the comforting words that Aaron is to be gathered to his people. Aaron was to join the number of believers whose souls had gone to heaven to await the great resurrection. Even as the Lord reminded Moses and Aaron about their sin at Kadesh, he included this beautiful term that pointed to the continued existence of people in heaven. As far as Aaron was concerned, "his people" who had died before were still alive and he could go and join them. The comfort in the resurrection of the dead and knowledge of continued existence in heaven existed already for the people of the Old Testament.

But prior to his death there was to be a solemn transfer of the office of high priest. In the sight of all the people the official high priestly garments were passed from Aaron to

Death of Aaron

his son, Eleazar. The ceremony was visible to the people as Aaron, Moses and Eleazar stood on the side of Mount Hor. We are told that Aaron died and only Moses and Eleazar returned from the mountain. In this way the Lord provided that there would be no break in the priesthood. The mediatorial work of the high priest was to go on without interruption.

In a demonstration of their respect the people spent thirty days in mourning for their first high priest. Such a tribute is indeed appropriate for a faithful servant of the Lord and is worthy of imitation by all children of God.

In a slow drumbeat of death, the leaders of Israel are dying. Yet as Aaron was told that it was time to die, we might at first think that it was unkind to tell him. On the other hand, he had the full assurance that the Lord had chosen exactly the right moment. That assurance is really the comfort that every Christian has at his death. Though death is a consequence of sin, the timing still takes place according to God's will. Further, because he sent the Savior, the grave is only the resting place of the body until the great day of the final resurrection.

Arad Destroyed

21 When the Canaanite king of Arad, who lived in the Negev, heard that Israel was coming along the road to Atharim, he attacked the Israelites and captured some of them. ²Then Israel made this vow to the Lord: "If you will deliver these people into our hands, we will totally destroy their cities." ³The Lord listened to Israel's plea and gave the Canaanites over to them. They completely destroyed them and their towns; so the place was named Hormah.

This incident records the warfare with which the Lord initiated destruction of the Canaanites. The people were from the kingdom of Arad, which was in the desert area (Negev) south of the land of Canaan.

When the king of Arad had heard of Israel's approach, he apparently attacked some of the outlying areas of the Israelite camp. He was successful in carrying some Israelites away into captivity. In spite of the fact that they faced such a provocation, we note how appropriately the Israelites responded. They indicated their willingness to attack Arad but asked the Lord to give them victory. They then promised that they would carry out a total destruction of the cities.

The Lord indicated his approval of the plan and gave the victory. The victory was so complete that the place received the name Hormah, which means "destruction." Yet there must have been some survivors or other branches of the clan. A complete destruction was reported later in Judges 1:16,17.

The Bronze Snake

4They traveled from Mount Hor along the route to the Red Sea, to go around Edom. But the people grew impatient on the way; 5they spoke against God and against Moses, and said, "Why have you brought us up out of Egypt to die in the desert? There is no bread! There is no water! And we detest this miserable food!"

6Then the LORD sent venomous snakes among them; they bit the people and many Israelites died. 7The people came to Moses and said, "We sinned when we spoke against the LORD and against you. Pray that the LORD will take the snakes away from us." So Moses prayed for the people.

8The LORD said to Moses, "Make a snake and put it up on a pole; anyone who is bitten can look at it and live." 9So Moses made a bronze snake and put it up on a pole. Then when anyone was bitten by a snake and looked at the bronze snake, he lived.

Because the king of Edom refused passage to the children of Israel, their route took them southward toward the Gulf of Aqaba and eastward toward the Arabian desert. Because the route was not the direct one, the people again began to murmur and complain. Even this generation, which was removed forty years from life in Egypt, repeated the complaints of the first generation. "Why did you take us away from Egypt, Moses? There is no bread or water here in the wilderness, and all we get is this miserable stuff that is called manna." In their complaining mood they were blind to the many gifts God was giving them.

To jar the people to their senses the Lord sent venomous snakes among them. Many died because they were bitten by the snakes. At this point the improved attitude of the new generation can be seen. They recognized the chastisement and confessed their sin of discontent. Therefore they appealed to the Lord through Moses. So Moses once again faithfully acted as the mediator between the people and the Lord. In answer to Moses' prayer God told Moses to set up a bronze snake. The Lord promised that anyone who looked toward the bronze snake would live. So Moses made a bronze snake, set up on a post where everyone could see it. The account closes with the notation that people were saved exactly in the way that the Lord had indicated. Those who believed the promise of the Lord and looked at the snake when they were bitten were saved.

This account is especially dear to people of the New Testament because Jesus pointed to it in John 3. The bronze snake prefigured Christ's crucifixion. Just as the Israelites were saved from the poison of the snakes when they looked in faith toward the bronze snake, so believers of all ages can look to Christ in faith and be saved from the spiritual poison of sin. The grace of God stands behind both situations so that those who believed God's promises were and will be saved. Jesus declared, "Just as Moses lifted up the snake in the desert, so the Son of Man must be lifted up, that everyone who believes in him may have eternal life. For God so loved the world that he gave his one and only Son, that whoever believes in him shall not perish but have eternal life" (John 3:14-16).

The Journey to Moab

[10]The Israelites moved on and camped at Oboth. [11]Then they set out from Oboth and camped in Iye Abarim, in the desert that faces Moab toward the sunrise. [12]From there they moved on and camped in the Zered Valley. [13]They set out from there and camped alongside the Arnon, which is in the desert extending into Amorite territory. The Arnon is the border of Moab, between Moab and the Amorites. [14]That is why the Book of the Wars of the LORD says:

> ". . . Waheb in Suphah and the ravines,
>   the Arnon [15]and the slopes of the ravines
> that lead to the site of Ar
>   and lie along the border of Moab."

[16]From there they continued on to Beer, the well where the LORD said to Moses, "Gather the people together and I will give them water."

[17]Then Israel sang this song:

> "Spring up, O well!
>   Sing about it,
> [18]about the well that the princes dug,
>   that the nobles of the people sank —
>   the nobles with scepters and staffs."

Then they went from the desert to Mattanah, [19]from Mattanah to Nahaliel, from Nahaliel to Bamoth, [20]and from Bamoth to the valley in Moab where the top of Pisgah overlooks the wasteland.

The account that Moses gives moves quickly through the final miles of the journey to the shores of the Jordan River. For the generation that had now come of age it must have been a thrilling journey. Half of them had never known anything but the austere landscapes of the wilderness. How exciting it must have been as they began to experience the lush fertility of the area around the Promised Land. What new beauties and new hope each day must have brought!

Various campsites are mentioned. The final one is described as being along the Arnon River, the border between the land of Moab and the Amorites. The remaining chapters of the book of Numbers record events that took place in the rectangle of land east of the Jordan River between the northern boundary of the Dead Sea and the southern boundary of the Sea of Galilee (Kinnereth).

Two special campsites are mentioned. In connection with one a poem was created to mark the event. Moses tells us that the poem came from the "Book of Wars," a book that has not survived to our times.

The second campsite (with the name Beer, which means "a water well") was also marked by a special song of joy that the people sang about the abundance of water that was supplied by the Lord there.

Another interesting word is "Bamoth." It is a descriptive name for a high place or fortress.

Defeat of Sihon and Og

21 Israel sent messengers to say to Sihon king of the Amorites:

22"Let us pass through your country. We will not turn aside into any field or vineyard, or drink water from any well. We will travel along the king's highway until we have passed through your territory."

23 But Sihon would not let Israel pass through his territory. He mustered his entire army and marched out into the desert against Israel. When he reached Jahaz, he fought with Israel. 24 Israel, however, put him to the sword and took over his land from the Arnon to the Jabbok, but only as far as the Ammonites, because

their border was fortified. ²⁵Israel captured all the cities of the Amorites and occupied them, including Heshbon and all its surrounding settlements. ²⁶Heshbon was the city of Sihon king of the Amorites, who had fought against the former king of Moab and had taken from him all his land as far as the Arnon.

²⁷That is why the poets say:

> "Come to Heshbon and let it be rebuilt;
> let Sihon's city be restored.

²⁸"Fire went out from Heshbon,
> a blaze from the city of Sihon.
> It consumed Ar of Moab,
> the citizens of Arnon's heights.

²⁹Woe to you, O Moab!
> You are destroyed, O people of Chemosh!
> He has given up his sons as fugitives
> and his daughters as captives
> to Sihon king of the Amorites.

³⁰"But we have overthrown them;
> Heshbon is destroyed all the way to Dibon.
> We have demolished them as far as Nophah,
> which extends to Medeba."

³¹So Israel settled in the land of the Amorites.

³²After Moses had sent spies to Jazer, the Israelites captured its surrounding settlements and drove out the Amorites who were there. ³³Then they turned and went up along the road toward Bashan, and Og king of Bashan and his whole army marched out to meet them in battle at Edrei.

³⁴The LORD said to Moses, "Do not be afraid of him, for I have handed him over to you, with his whole army and his land. Do to him what you did to Sihon king of the Amorites, who reigned in Heshbon."

³⁵So they struck him down, together with his sons and his whole army, leaving them no survivors. And they took possession of his land.

As on previous occasions, the Israelites were instructed to request permission to pass through the territory of King

Sihon. The request was denied. The Amorites, however, were not under the Lord's protection as the Edomites and Moabites had been. In this case it was the Lord's intention to use the children of Israel as his weapon to punish the people of Canaan. The Israelites were to attack Sihon when he gathered his army and moved against them at Jahaz. Following the Lord's marching orders, the children of Israel were granted a great victory at Jahaz. In the mopping up operation that followed, they took control of the whole area from the Arnon to the Jabbok, including the capital city, Heshbon. Under the Lord's blessing the victory was overwhelming.

The poetry reflects the total victory. The poem has three parts. The first part points to the utter defeat of the Amorites under Sihon. The second part is a boast and a taunt toward Moab, because Sihon had defeated Moab earlier and now the Israelites had defeated Sihon. The third part restates the complete victory of Israel.

The next military engagement focused on Jazer, to which spies had been sent. After capturing Jazer, the Israelites were directed to attack Og, the king of Bashan. The landscape of this country was like the long sloping hills of the great Plains in the United States. Battle was joined at Edrei. The Lord had promised victory and had commanded that there should be no survivors. The children of Israel were obedient and as a result they captured another large tract of land. The Israelites were now in complete control of the rectangle of land east of the Jordan that stretches from the Sea of Galilee in the north to the Dead Sea in the south. The Lord had made a down payment on his promise to give his chosen people the land that flowed with milk and honey.

These events give us every reason to believe that the LORD has the strength to conquer all his enemies. Whenever we see God's mighty hand in victory, may we gladly give thanks to him for his mercy and for his faithfulness to his promise.

FROM KADESH TO THE JORDAN

Life in the Community

The second portion of this part of Numbers which we have entitled "From Kadesh to the Jordan" shows us that God protects not only from armies but also from false prophets. One can be as dangerous as the other, as Satan tries to mislead the people of God. Balaam, a greedy prophet, was summoned to curse the children of Israel. The Lord prevented him from carrying out his purpose. But the greedy prophet then suggested to the king of Moab that the Israelites should be seduced into idolatry. This ploy was quite successful. The section closes with the second census of the people, which showed that the Israelites who were twenty years old or more at the time of the crossing of the Red Sea were dead.

Balak Summons Balaam

22 **Then the Israelites traveled to the plains of Moab and camped along the Jordan across from Jericho.**

²Now Balak son of Zippor saw all that Israel had done to the Amorites, ³and Moab was terrified because there were so many people. Indeed, Moab was filled with dread because of the Israelites.

⁴The Moabites said to the elders of Midian, "This horde is going to lick up everything around us, as an ox licks up the grass of the field."

So Balak son of Zippor, who was king of Moab at that time, ⁵sent messengers to summon Balaam son of Beor, who was at Pethor, near the River, in his native land. Balak said:

"A people has come out of Egypt; they cover the face of the land and have settled next to me. ⁶Now come and put a curse on these people, because they are too powerful for me. Perhaps then I will be able to defeat them and drive them out of the country. For I know that those you bless are blessed, and those you curse are cursed."

⁷The elders of Moab and Midian left, taking with them the fee for divination. When they came to Balaam, they told him what Balak had said.

⁸"Spend the night here," Balaam said to them, "and I will bring you back the answer the LORD gives me." So the Moabite princes stayed with him.

⁹God came to Balaam and asked, "Who are these men with you?"

¹⁰Balaam said to God, "Balak son of Zippor, king of Moab, sent me this message: ¹¹'A people that has come out of Egypt covers the face of the land. Now come and put a curse on them for me. Perhaps then I will be able to fight them and drive them away.' "

¹²But God said to Balaam, "Do not go with them. You must not put a curse on those people, because they are blessed."

¹³The next morning Balaam got up and said to Balak's princes, "Go back to your own country, for the LORD has refused to let me go with you."

¹⁴So the Moabite princes returned to Balak and said, "Balaam refused to come with us."

¹⁵Then Balak sent other princes, more numerous and more distinguished than the first. ¹⁶They came to Balaam and said:

"This is what Balak son of Zippor says: Do not let anything keep you from coming to me, ¹⁷because I will reward you handsomely and do whatever you say. Come and put a curse on these people for me."

¹⁸But Balaam answered them, "Even if Balak gave me his palace filled with silver and gold, I could not do anything great or small to go beyond the command of the LORD my God. ¹⁹Now

stay here tonight as the others did, and I will find out what else the LORD will tell me.

²⁰That night God came to Balaam and said, "Since these men have come to summon you, go with them, but do only what I tell you."

The king of Moab was upset and frightened. A huge mass of people, the children of Israel, had wandered past his land on the east. Then they had moved westward and conquered the neighboring kingdoms of Sihon and Og. One of those nations, the Amorites under King Sihon, had been powerful enough to defeat Moab earlier. The king of Moab panicked when he saw this army of invaders parked on his northern border. Under such circumstances the king of Moab needed something more than armies. In a vivid comparison the king described the Israelites like cattle eating all the grass before them. With so many people so close the king of Moab felt as helpless as grass.

And so, in league with the Midianites, Balak the king of Moab sent messengers to Mesopotamia, to a prophet named Balaam. To the pagan mind of Balak it seemed that the only chance he had against the children of Israel was to have some accredited diviner place a curse on them.

King Balak was referred to Balaam, who could probably be compared to a specialist in world religions in our contemporary universities. Balaam probably claimed some expertise in the religion of the Israelites, since he used the special covenant name of the true God (note the places in the NIV text where the capitalized LORD is used).

When the messengers arrived at Balaam's home they presented the request of their king. The prophet invited them to stay overnight since he would have to wait for an answer from the Lord. Balaam may very well not even have expected the Lord to answer. Since he used the proper name,

"LORD," some people have assumed that he was a prophet of the true God. More likely Balaam considered the "LORD" no more than one of many gods.

It suited the Lord's purpose to communicate with Balaam. He came to Balaam that night. He flatly forbade Balaam to go with the messengers. Balaam was warned. To God it was an insult for Balaam to go and place a curse on a people who were blessed by the true God.

The next morning Balaam sent the messengers away, hinting that if it were his own choice he would have gladly come. It was the Lord who had refused to let him go. The conniving of Balaam surfaced when he did not include the explanation, namely, that the Lord had blessed the Israelites and therefore no one could curse them. Such an explanation would have immediately cut off any hope of further negotiations.

Assuming that Balaam would be persuaded to come if there were more in it for him, King Balak persisted. He sent messengers, who were more noble, and promised greater rewards. To this second group of messengers Balaam expressed the disclaimer that riches would not influence him in any way. He could not do anything great or small that went beyond what the Lord would tell him to do.

At the same time he made it very clear to his Moabite visitors that he was interested in their proposition. He invited the messengers to stay overnight while he would see what else the Lord might tell him. At this point Balaam was acting in a normal way for pagan soothsayers. He hoped that he could influence the Lord in some way and thus gain permission to go with the messengers. He was approaching the situation with the question: "Can't I go a little further, Lord?" That question and the attitude that is behind it has been the downfall of many a person, just as it was the downfall of Balaam.

Balaam and the Donkey

Surprisingly, the Lord did appear to Balaam again that night. He told this defiant pagan: "All right, go with them. But do only what I tell you." God's permission was already a judgment on this stubborn heathen, who knew that the Lord was blessing the children of Israel. Therefore it was futile for Balaam to hope that he would be allowed to curse them as Balak wanted. Yet Balaam proceeded blithely into a trap which had no escape: Balak wanted him to curse Israel; God would compel him to bless Israel.

Balaam's Donkey

²¹Balaam got up in the morning, saddled his donkey and went with the princes of Moab. ²²But God was very angry when he went, and the angel of the LORD stood in the road to oppose him. Balaam was riding on his donkey, and his two servants were with him. ²³When the donkey saw the angel of the LORD standing in the road with a drawn sword in his hand, she turned off the road into a field. Balaam beat her to get her back on the road.

²⁴Then the angel of the LORD stood in a narrow path between two vineyards, with walls on both sides. ²⁵When the donkey saw the angel of the LORD, she pressed close to the wall, crushing Balaam's foot against it. So he beat her again.

²⁶Then the angel of the LORD moved on ahead and stood in a narrow place where there was no room to turn, either to the right or to the left. ²⁷When the donkey saw the angel of the LORD, she lay down under Balaam, and he was angry and beat her with his staff. ²⁸Then the LORD opened the donkey's mouth, and she said to Balaam, "What have I done to you to make you beat me these three times?"

²⁹Balaam answered the donkey, "You have made a fool of me! If I had a sword in my hand, I would kill you right now."

³⁰The donkey said to Balaam, "Am I not your own donkey, which you have always ridden, to this day? Have I been in the habit of doing this to you?"

"No," he said.

31 Then the LORD opened Balaam's eyes, and he saw the angel of the LORD standing in the road with his sword drawn. So he bowed low and fell facedown.

32 The angel of the LORD asked him, "Why have you beaten your donkey these three times? I have come here to oppose you because your path is a reckless one before me. **33** The donkey saw me and turned away from me these three times. If she had not turned away, I would certainly have killed you by now, but I would have spared her."

34 Balaam said to the angel of the LORD, "I have sinned. I did not realize you were standing in the road to oppose me. Now if you are displeased, I will go back."

35 The angel of the LORD said to Balaam, "Go with the men, but speak only what I tell you." So Balaam went with the princes of Balak.

36 When Balak heard that Balaam was coming, he went out to meet him at the Moabite town on the Arnon border, at the edge of his territory. **37** Balak said to Balaam, "Did I not send you an urgent summons? Why didn't you come to me? Am I really not able to reward you?"

38 "Well, I have come to you now," Balaam replied. "But can I say just anything? I must speak only what God puts in my mouth."

39 Then Balaam went with Balak to Kiriath Huzoth. **40** Balak sacrificed cattle and sheep, and gave some to Balaam and the princes who were with him. **41** The next morning Balak took Balaam up to Bamoth Baal, and from there he saw part of the people.

Balaam was without excuse. He had already been told twice that the children of Israel were blessed. Balaam had also been told that he should speak only what the Lord told him. But just in case Balaam had not been listening carefully the balkiness of a frightened donkey and the appearance of the Angel of the Lord were to give him the message once more in a manner he couldn't ignore.

Balaam was proceeding on the premise that he would see how far he could go with the Lord. By so doing he provoked the Lord. Yet the Lord was willing to let him go forward because the Lord was going to use Balaam for his purposes. Willing or unwilling, Balaam was going to pronounce a blessing upon the children of Israel.

Just so God could be sure that he had Balaam's attention, the Angel of the Lord appeared three times in front of his donkey. The first time the donkey turned off the road; the second time it pressed against the wall at the side of the road and crushed Balaam's foot; and the third time it lay down. Each time Balaam beat the donkey, because the Lord did not allow him at that time to see the Angel.

As Balaam beat his donkey for the third time, the Lord performed one of his most amazing miracles: he gave the voiceless donkey the ability to speak. The Lord was able to communicate even through this animal. So the donkey chided its master for his cruelty. Only then did Balaam see the Angel of the Lord on the path. The Angel then said, "Your path is a reckless one. If she had not turned away, I would have killed you by now." The donkey had really saved his life. At this Balaam indicated that he recognized his sin and that he would turn back if the Angel told him to do so. In his answer Balaam continued to show that he still wanted to try to finagle something out of the situation. The Angel then allowed him to go forward but very emphatically said, "Speak only what I tell you."

Because the Angel spoke here and repeated the earlier commands of God, he identified himself with God. So we must conclude that this Angel is the second person of the Trinity. Centuries before he appeared in human form in Bethlehem he appeared as the Angel of the Lord a number of times in the Old Testament.

In spite of God's repeated warnings, Balaam traveled on. He reached the land of Moab, where he met King Balak. It had been so clearly impressed on his mind that he was to speak only the will of God that he immediately pointed out that fact to Balak when they met.

As the Son of God prevented Balaam from carrying out his evil intention of cursing God's people, so our Savior now strengthens and upholds his church in all its trials and keeps its enemies from doing any lasting harm. "I will build my church, and the gates of Hades will not overcome it," our Savior has promised (Matthew 16:18).

It's ironic — instructive, too — that this victory of the Lord was about to occur at a place that was named "Bamoth Baal," that is, *the high place* or *citadel of Baal!*

Balaam's First Oracle

23 Balaam said, "Build me seven altars here, and prepare seven bulls and seven rams for me." ²Balak did as Balaam said, and the two of them offered a bull and a ram on each altar.

³Then Balaam said to Balak, "Stay here beside your offering while I go aside. Perhaps the LORD will come to meet with me. Whatever he reveals to me I will tell you." Then he went off to a barren height.

⁴God met with him, and Balaam said, "I have prepared seven altars, and on each altar I have offered a bull and a ram."

⁵The LORD put a message in Balaam's mouth and said, "Go back to Balak and give him this message."

⁶So he went back to him and found him standing beside his offering, with all the princes of Moab. ⁷Then Balaam uttered his oracle:

> "Balak brought me from Aram,
>> the king of Moab from the eastern mountains.
> 'Come,' he said, 'curse Jacob for me;
>> come, denounce Israel.'

8How can I curse
  those whom God has not cursed?
 How can I denounce
  those whom the LORD has not denounced?
9From the rocky peaks I see them,
  from the heights I view them.
 I see a people who live apart
  and do not consider themselves one of the nations.
10Who can count the dust of Jacob
  or number the fourth part of Israel?
 Let me die the death of the righteous,
  and may my end be like theirs!"

11Balak said to Balaam, "What have you done to me? I brought you to curse my enemies, but you have done nothing but bless them!"

12He answered, "Must I not speak what the LORD puts in my mouth?"

Balaam, the soothsayer, was getting in deeper and deeper. Balak, the king, was pushing him to pronounce a curse on God's people. Balaam gave instructions and joined Balak in making sacrifices. This sacrifice was an abomination to the Lord. It was an attempt to meld or blend the worship of idols with the worship of the true God. This practice is called syncretism. Such worship is a sin against the First Commandment because it places idols on an equal footing with the true God.

To give the procedure the appearance of correctness, Balaam used the number seven, which in the Scripture is considered the number of completeness or perfection. But the Lord was not duped. He was still in control. After the seven sacrifices had been made, Balaam moved away to a barren height in order to await God's message. When the Lord communicated with Balaam he reminded him to speak only the message that he had received from God. Note that

181

God was here communicating as the God of the Covenant, that is, the LORD. It was the LORD who put an oracle into Balaam's mouth.

The oracle had a brief introduction, reviewing Balaam's purpose. As a second point Balaam asked, "How can I curse those whom God has blessed?" Then he declared that they were a distinctive people, who had been set apart from the other nations. Finally, he prophesied vast numbers for Israel and closed with the prayer that he might die with Israel the death of the righteous.

For obvious reasons Balak was amazed and angry. But the king was desperately hoping that another time and another place would make it possible for Balaam to curse the people.

How clearly the Lord displayed his almighty power in opposition to the powers of heathenism! Even as they assembled to contend against Israel, the Lord showed his supremacy in disclosing his eternal purpose, using a person who was quite passive in his hand to disclose his eternal purpose.

Balaam's Second Oracle

¹³**Then Balak said to him, "Come with me to another place where you can see them; you will see only a part but not all of them. And from there, curse them for me." ¹⁴So he took him to the field of Zophim on the top of Pisgah, and there he built seven altars and offered a bull and a ram on each altar.**

¹⁵**Balaam said to Balak, "Stay here beside your offering while I meet with him over there."**

¹⁶**The Lord met with Balaam and put a message in his mouth and said, "Go back to Balak and give him this message."**

¹⁷**So he went to him and found him standing beside his offering, with the princes of Moab. Balak asked him, "What did the Lord say?"**

¹⁸**Then he uttered his oracle:**

"Arise, Balak, and listen;
>hear me, son of Zippor.
[19]God is not a man, that he should lie,
>not a son of man, that he should change his mind.
Does he speak and then not act?
>Does he promise and not fulfill?
[20]I have received a command to bless;
>he has blessed, and I cannot change it.
[21]"No misfortune is seen in Jacob,
>no misery observed in Israel.
The LORD their God is with them;
>the shout of the King is among them.
[22]God brought them out of Egypt;
>they have the strength of a wild ox.
[23]There is no sorcery against Jacob.
>no divination against Israel.
It will now be said of Jacob
>and of Israel, 'See what God has done!'
[24]The people rise like a lioness;
>they rouse themselves like a lion
that does not rest till he devours his prey
>and drinks the blood of his victims."

[25]Then Balak said to Balaam, "Neither curse them at all nor bless them at all!"

[26]Balaam answered, "Did I not tell you I must do whatever the LORD says?"

A change in time and place produced no change in God's will. Following the same sacrificial procedures Balaam separated himself from Balak and received another message from the Lord. The oracle is made up of five four-line stanzas, in which the last two lines always give the ground or basis for the declaration of the first two lines. (In stanza four the last two lines are quite long, so that in print they run over from one line to the other.)

183

This oracle of Balaam makes the following points:

1. Balak is urged to listen — God does not change his mind!
2. God does not speak a promise futilely — and he has blessed!
3. Misfortune will not afflict Israel — the Lord is with them!
4. God brought them out of Egypt — see what God has done!
5. They rise like a lion — and will devour their prey!

Balak's fuse has gotten short. If Balaam can't curse the Israelites, then, at least, he ought not bless them. Maybe better yet — Balaam should be quiet! Yet Balaam noted again that he could do only what the Lord commanded him.

Balaam's Third Oracle

²⁷Then Balak said to Balaam, "Come, let me take you to another place. Perhaps it will please God to let you curse them for me from there." ²⁸And Balak took Balaam to the top of Peor, overlooking the wasteland.

²⁹Balaam said, "Build me seven altars here, and prepare seven bulls and seven rams for me." ³⁰Balak did as Balaam had said, and offered a bull and a ram on each altar.

24 Now when Balaam saw that it pleased the Lord to bless Israel, he did not resort to sorcery as at other times, but turned his face toward the desert. ²When Balaam looked out and saw Israel encamped tribe by tribe, the Spirit of God came upon him ³and he uttered his oracle:

"The oracle of Balaam son of Beor,
    the oracle of one whose eye sees clearly,
⁴the oracle of one who hears the words of God,
    who sees a vision from the Almighty,
    who falls prostrate, and whose eyes are opened:
⁵"How beautiful are your tents, O Jacob,
    your dwelling places, O Israel!

⁶"Like valleys they spread out,
    like gardens beside a river,
like aloes planted by the LORD,
    like cedars beside the waters.
⁷Water will flow from their buckets;
    their seed will have abundant water.

"Their king will be greater than Agag;
    their kingdom will be exalted.

⁸"God brought them out of Egypt;
    they have the strength of a wild ox.
They devour hostile nations
    and break their bones in pieces;
    with their arrows they pierce them.
⁹Like a lion they crouch and lie down,
    like a lioness — who dares to rouse them?

"May those who bless you be blessed
    and those who curse you be cursed!"

¹⁰Then Balak's anger burned against Balaam. He struck his hands together and said to him, "I summoned you to curse my enemies, but you have blessed them these three times. ¹¹Now leave at once and go home! I said I would reward you handsomely, but the LORD has kept you from being rewarded."

¹²Balaam answered Balak, "Did I not tell the messengers you sent me, ¹³'Even if Balak gave me his palace filled with silver and gold, I could not do anything of my own accord, good or bad, to go beyond the command of the LORD — and I must say only what the LORD says'? ¹⁴Now I am going back to my people, but come, let me warn you of what this people will do to your people in days to come."

There is a note at the beginning of this section that Balaam no longer resorted to the sorcery that he had tried to use earlier. Instead the Lord took complete control of this unwilling prophet and the Spirit of God entered him.

This third oracle emphasized the following truths:

1. Balaam's oracle — he speaks in a trance with his eyes open.
2. He beholds the beauty of the camp — the rows of tents like a garden.
3. Prosperity for Israel — with water and having a king.
4. God brought Israel out — now they are an ox, an army, a lion!
5. The blessing of Abraham also applies to them.

By this time Balak had had it! He withdrew the rewards he had offered and told Balaam to leave. Balaam, of course, hid behind the fact that he had to do what the Lord told him to do, as he had said previously. But the Lord was not yet finished with Balaam. Under the Lord's influence Balaam was to issue further oracles, some of which were further bad news to Balak, but good news for God's people.

Balaam's Fourth Oracle

¹⁵Then he uttered his oracle:

"The oracle of Balaam son of Beor,
  the oracle of one whose eye sees clearly,
¹⁶the oracle of one who hears the words of God,
  who has knowledge from the Most High,
who sees a vision from the Almighty,
  who falls prostrate, and whose eyes are opened:
¹⁷"I see him, but not now;
  I behold him, but not near.
A star will come out of Jacob;
  a scepter will rise out of Israel.
He will crush the foreheads of Moab,
  the skulls of all the sons of Sheth.
¹⁸Edom will be conquered;
  Seir, his enemy, will be conquered,
  but Israel will grow strong.

¹⁹A ruler will come out of Jacob
and destroy the survivors of the city."

In this unrequested oracle Balaam's prophecies reach
their climax. Balaam described himself as one who under
God's influence could see clearly. The Lord had fully
instructed him, while he was in a trance. The second verse
points to the coming Messiah, whom he sees, "not now . . .
not near." The Messiah arising out of Israel, will be like a
star and have a scepter. The next part of the prophecy seems
to telescope the time of David, who was a great earthly king,
with the time of the Messiah. Moab will be crushed; Edom
will be conquered. This ruler will come from Israel and
conquer both physically and spiritually.

The key words for Balak were God's solemn warning that
Moab would be crushed.

Balaam's Final Oracles

²⁰Then Balaam saw Amalek and uttered his oracle:
"Amalek was first among the nations,
but he will come to ruin at last."
²¹Then he saw the Kenites and uttered his oracle:
"Your dwelling place is secure,
your nest is set in a rock;
²²yet you Kenites will be destroyed
when Asshur takes you captive."
²³Then he uttered his oracle:
"Ah, who can live when God does this?
²⁴   Ships will come from the shores of Kittim;
they will subdue Asshur and Eber,
but they too will come to ruin."
²⁵Then Balaam got up and returned home and Balak went his
own way.

Balaam's visit to Moab was concluded with more un-solicited oracles.

Amalek, which had been the first nation to attack Israel in the Sinai peninsula, would sink from being the first into utter ruination.

The Kenites, a nation that was kind to Israel, would survive until Asshur (Assyria) conquered the whole region.

Ships from Kittim, which was a way of referring to the western lands of the Mediterranean basin, would destroy both Asshur and Eber and in turn that nation would be destroyed. This seems to be a very clear prophecy looking forward almost 1,500 years to the time of the Roman Em-pire. Truly the Lord did use Balaam, treacherous as he was, for his own purposes in disclosing the future.

After Balaam finished his oracles, he returned to his home in Mesopotamia. Apparently he came back fairly quickly because we will soon meet him again among the Midianites.

Balaam, the puzzling soothsayer, is mentioned several other times in the Scripture. Even though he was not al-lowed to pronounce a curse on the children of Israel, ap-parently he tried his best to serve Balak in an effort to get the reward. He had tried to turn Jehovah away from his people. The next plan proposed by Balaam was to turn the people away from Jehovah. From Numbers 31:16 and Revelation 2:14 we learn Balaam advised Balak to lead the children of Israel into idolatry and adultery connected with the worship of idols. Adultery as a form of idol worship was common among the Moabites and Midianites. With this devilish advice Balaam succeeded. Some of the people did turn from their God. It was Balaam's advice that led to the problem and the judgment of God that is described in the next chapter.

Moab Seduces Israel

25 While Israel was staying in Shittim, the men began to indulge in sexual immorality with Moabite women, ²who invited them to the sacrifices to their gods. The people ate and bowed down before these gods. ³So Israel joined in worshiping the Baal of Peor. And the LORD's anger burned against them.

⁴The LORD said to Moses, "Take all the leaders of these people, kill them and expose them in broad daylight before the LORD, so that the LORD's fierce anger may turn away from Israel."

⁵So Moses said to Israel's judges, "Each of you must put to death those of your men who have joined in worshiping the Baal of Peor."

⁶Then an Israelite man brought to his family a Midianite woman right before the eyes of Moses and the whole assembly of Israel while they were weeping at the entrance to the Tent of Meeting. ⁷When Phinehas son of Eleazar, the son of Aaron, the priest, saw this he left the assembly, took a spear in his hand ⁸and followed the Israelite into the tent. He drove the spear through both of them — through the Israelite and into the woman's body. Then the plague against the Israelites was stopped; ⁹but those who died in the plague numbered 24,000.

¹⁰The LORD said to Moses, ¹¹"Phinehas son of Eleazar, the son of Aaron, the priest, has turned my anger away from the Israelites; for he was as zealous as I am for my honor among them, so that in my zeal I did not put an end to them. ¹²Therefore tell him I am making my covenant of peace with him. ¹³He and his descendants will have a covenant of a lasting priesthood, because he was zealous for the honor of his God and made atonement for the Israelites."

¹⁴The name of the Israelite who was killed with the Midianite woman was Zimri son of Salu, the leader of a Simeonite family. ¹⁵And the name of the Midianite woman who was put to death was Cozbi daughter of Zur, a tribal chief of a Midianite family.

¹⁶The LORD said to Moses, ¹⁷"Treat the Midianites as enemies and kill them, ¹⁸because they treated you as enemies when they

deceived you in the affair of Peor and their sister Cozbi, the daughter of a Midianite leader, the woman who was killed when the plague came as a result of Peor."

Balaam could not curse Israel! Yet he tried to make some money by giving advice to the Midianites and Moabites. He suggested they entice the Israelites to join them in their idolatrous and adulterous worship of Baal, the Canaanite god of fertility. Though the text does not specifically refer to Balaam here, the deceptive actions of that soothsayer provides the connection between this chapter and the previous chapters. Following Balaam's advice the Moabites and Midianites tempted the children of Israel to join in the immoral orgies with which they worshipped their idols. The siren plea was: "Our gods are as good as your gods, so come on over. We have a lot more fun worshiping our gods." Some of the Israelites were enticed into idolatrous worship as they rationalized that one way of worshiping God is probably as good as another.

But God will not be mocked. He will not share the honor that he alone deserves. He is offended even when people claim to worship him under man-made names. Therefore the Lord addressed Moses. He indicated his anger and gave the command that the leaders should proceed according to the laws they had received. God's laws gave the leaders of Israel the responsibility to execute people who were guilty of either idolatry or adultery. In the current situation the people were guilty of both sins. The leaders were to identify the offenders, execute them, and expose the whole shameful thing to the light of day. Only with stern action could the anger of the Lord be turned away.

In obedience to the Lord Moses assigned the judges and gave them the firm orders to put to death anyone who had joined in worshiping Baal of Peor.

While this judgment was in process, a brazen example of adultery took place before the eyes of the leaders. A man of Israel brought a Midianite woman into the camp and took her into his tent right before his own family. Indeed, the man was so bold that he did not even try to hide his intention from the leaders as they stood at the Tent of Meeting.

Thinking quickly, the priest Phinehas took a spear and followed the man into the tent. He drove his spear right through both the man and the woman. Normally such a violent act was forbidden to the high priest. But against gross idolatry and adultery Phinehas was indeed acting on behalf of a righteous God. His act actually saved the people from further anger of God. We are told that with Phinehas's act of righteous indignation the plague stopped. It should be noted that 24,000 died in this plague. The Lord will not be mocked either by adultery or idolatry.

The zeal of Phinehas had turned the anger of the Lord away. God then promised Phinehas in a covenant that the priesthood would remain in his family.

This chapter ends with the note that the name of the Israelite was Zimri. The woman was named Cozbi. She was a daughter of Zur, a tribal chieftain of the Midianites. These facts measure the total effort of Midianite society to mislead the Israelites. In answer to such hostility the Lord instructed the children of Israel to treat the Midianites as enemies, even though they were descendants of Abraham (see Genesis 25:2).

The Second Census

26 After the plague the LORD said to Moses and Eleazar son of Aaron, the priest, [2]"Take a census of the whole Israelite community by families — all those twenty years old or more who are able to serve in the army of Israel." [3]So on the plains of Moab by the Jordan across from Jericho, Moses and Eleazar the priest spoke with them and said, [4]"Take a census of the men twenty years old or more, as the LORD commanded Moses."

These were the Israelites who came out of Egypt:

[5]The descendants of Reuben, the firstborn son of Israel, were:

through Hanoch, the Hanochite clan;

through Pallu, the Palluite clan;

[6]through Hezron, the Hezronite clan;

through Carmi, the Carmite clan.

[7]These were the clans of Reuben; those numbered were 43,730.

[8]The son of Pallu was Eliab, [9]and the sons of Eliab were Nemuel, Dathan and Abiram. The same Dathan and Abiram were the community officials who rebelled against Moses and Aaron and were among Korah's followers when they rebelled against the LORD. [10]The earth opened its mouth and swallowed them along with Korah, whose followers died when the fire devoured the 250 men. And they served as a warning sign. [11]The line of Korah, however, did not die out.

[12]The descendants of Simeon by their clans were:

through Nemuel, the Nemuelite clan;

through Jamin, the Jaminite clan;

through Jakin, the Jakinite clan;

[13]through Zerah, the Zerahite clan;

through Shaul, the Shaulite clan.

[14]These were the clans of Simeon; there were 22,200 men.

[15]The descendants of Gad by their clans were:

through Zephon, the Zephonite clan;

through Haggi, the Haggite clan;

through Shuni, the Shunite clan;

[16]through Ozni, the Oznite clan;

through Eri, the Erite clan;

[17]through Arodi, the Arodite clan;

through Areli, the Arelite clan.

[18]These were the clans of Gad; those numbered were 40,500.

[19]Er and Onan were sons of Judah, but they died in Canaan.

[20]The descendants of Judah by their clans were:

through Shelah, the Shelanite clan;
through Perez, the Perezite clan;
through Zerah, the Zerahite clan.
²¹The descendants of Perez were:
through Hezron, the Hezronite clan;
through Hamul, the Hamulite clan.
²²These were the clans of Judah; those numbered were 76,500.
²³The descendants of Issachar by their clans were:
through Tola, the Tolaite clan;
through Puah, the Puite clan;
²⁴through Jashub, the Jashubite clan;
through Shimron, the Shimronite clan.
²⁵These were the clans of Issachar; those numbered were 64,300.
²⁶The descendants of Zebulun by their clans were:
through Sered, the Seredite clan;
through Elon, the Elonite clan;
through Jahleel, the Jahleelite clan.
²⁷These were the clans of Zebulun; those numbered were 60,500.
²⁸The descendants of Joseph by their clans through Manasseh and Ephraim were:
²⁹The descendants of Manasseh:
through Makir, the Makirite clan (Makir was the father of Gilead);
through Gilead, the Gileadite clan;
³⁰These were the descendants of Gilead:
through Iezer, the Iezerite clan;
through Helek, the Helekite clan;
³¹through Asriel, the Asrielite clan;
through Shechem, the Shechemite clan;
³²through Shemida, the Shemidaite clan;
through Hepher, the Hepherite clan;
³³(Zelophehad son of Hepher had no sons; he had only daughters, whose names were Mahlah, Noah, Hoglah, Milcah and Tirzah.)
³⁴These were the clans of Manasseh; those numbered were 52,700.

³⁵The descendants of Ephraim by their clans were:
    through Shuthelah, the Shuthelahite clan;
    through Beker, the Bekerite clan;
    through Tahan, the Tahanite clan.
  ³⁶These were the descendants of Shuthelah:
    through Eran, the Eranite clan.

³⁷These were the clans of Ephraim; those numbered were 32,500.

These were the descendants of Joseph by their clans.

³⁸The descendants of Benjamin by their clans were:
    through Bela, the Belaite clan;
    through Ashbel, the Ashbelite clan;
    through Ahiram, the Ahiramite clan;
  ³⁹through Shupham, the Shuphamite clan;
    through Hupham, the Huphamite clan.
  ⁴⁰The descendants of Bela through Ard and Naaman were:
    through Ard, the Ardite clan;
    through Naaman, the Naamite clan.

⁴¹These were the clans of Benjamin; those numbered were 45,600.

⁴²These were the descendants of Dan by their clans:
    through Shuham, the Shuhamite clan.

These were the clans of Dan: ⁴³All of them were Shuhamite clans; and those numbered were 64,400.

⁴⁴The descendants of Asher by their clans were:
    through Imnah, the Imnite clan;
    through Ishvi, the Ishvite clan;
    through Beriah, the Beriite clan;
  ⁴⁵and through the descendants of Beriah:
    through Heber, the Heberite clan;
    through Malkiel, the Malkielite clan.
  ⁴⁶(Asher had a daughter named Serah.)

⁴⁷These were the clans of Asher; those numbered were 53,400.

⁴⁸The descendants of Naphtali by their clans were:
    through Jahzeel, the Jahzeelite clan;
    through Guni, the Gunite clan;
  ⁴⁹through Jezer, the Jezerite clan;

through Shillem, the Shillemite clan.
⁵⁰These were the clans of Naphtali; those numbered were 45,400.
⁵¹The total number of the men of Israel was 601,730.

⁵²The LORD said to Moses, ⁵³"The land is to be allotted to them as an inheritance based on the number of names. ⁵⁴To a larger group give a larger inheritance, and to a smaller group a smaller one; each is to receive its inheritance according to the number of those listed. ⁵⁵Be sure that the land is distributed by lot. What each group inherits will be according to the names for its ancestral tribe. ⁵⁶Each inheritance is to be distributed by lot among the larger and smaller groups."

⁵⁷These were the Levites who were counted by their clans:
through Gershon, the Gershonite clan;
through Kohath, the Kohathite clan;
through Merari, the Merarite clan.
⁵⁸These also were Levite clans:
the Libnite clan,
the Hebronite clan,
the Mahlite clan,
the Mushite clan,
the Korahite clan.
(Kohath was the forefather of Amran; ⁵⁹the name of Amran's wife was Jochebed, a descendant of Levi, who was born to the Levites in Egypt. To Amram she bore Aaron, Moses and their sister Miriam. ⁶⁰Aaron was the father of Nadab and Abihu, Eleazar and Ithamar. ⁶¹But Nadab and Abihu died when they made an offering before the LORD with unauthorized fire.)

⁶²All the male Levites a month old or more numbered 23,000. They were not counted along with the other Israelites because they received no inheritance among them.

⁶³These are the ones counted by Moses and Eleazar the priest when they counted the Israelites on the plains of Moab by the Jordan across from Jericho. ⁶⁴Not one of them was among those counted by Moses and Aaron the priest when they counted the Israelites in the Desert of Sinai. ⁶⁵For the LORD had told those

Israelites they would surely die in the desert, and not one of them was left except Caleb son of Jephunneh and Joshua son of Nun.

The children of Israel were encamped on the east side of the Jordan River. They could look across the river into the Promised Land. At this point the Lord commanded that a second census be taken. This census, like the earlier one, could more properly be called a mustering, since only the men twenty years old and over who were fit for military service were counted. Once again the tribes and families arranged themselves, and the totals were determined.

The total number of people was 601,730. This is a very small decrease from the 603,550 that had been counted in the first mustering (see chapter 1.) Normally one would have expected the nation to grow in numbers over a thirty-eight year period. For the nation instead to have shrunk in size shows clearly that other than natural causes were at work here.

A closer examination of individual tribal totals shows that the tribe of Reuben had lost a sizable proportion of people. This reminds, us, first of all, that the rebellion of Dathan and Abiram had especially involved the Reubenites. It would therefore follow that the tribe must have lost a large number of people at that time. Similarly, the tribe of Simeon had shrunk from 59,300 to 22,300. This shocking loss of sixty percent of its able-bodied men may be traceable in part to the recent plague (see 25:9,14). On the other hand, Judah was the tribe that carried the promise of the Savior. Therefore it pleased God to allow that tribe to grow more rapidly.

By demanding this census the Lord meant to remind the people that he had kept his promises — Balaam, Midian and Moab notwithstanding.

196

Another of God's purposes looked forward to the entry into the Promised Land. Through this mustering the people would be better able to determine how the land in Canaan was to be apportioned among the twelve tribes. Instructions were given that the land was to be assigned by lot to the men who were numbered at this time. Furthermore, the Lord had determined that each tribe was to receive territory in proportion to its size. So this census also indicated how much territory would be necessary for each of the tribes.

A census of the Levites was also taken. Special notes were added concerning the lineage of Aaron, Moses and Miriam. The total number of Levites was 23,000. Over the years in the wilderness the number of Levites had remained virtually unchanged, even though 250 Levite men had died in the rebellion of Korah.

A final purpose of this census is given in the last sentences of the chapter. The Lord was looking back to the fateful day when the children of Israel had failed to go forward under the blessing of the Lord, because of the fears inspired by the report of the ten spies. At that time the Lord said that not one of the people who had been counted in the desert of Sinai would be allowed to enter the Promised Land. Therefore at the conclusion of this census there is the solemn statement that, except for Caleb and Joshua, not one person who was alive when the Israelites were counted at Sinai was still living. The two exceptions by their very existence made the point most emphatically that God is faithful! God had promised! Those two had urged the children of Israel to go forward. In faith they had said, "The LORD is with us." Therefore God had specifically promised that the two of them would have their own inheritance in the land of milk and honey. The Lord would keep this promise also!

FROM KADESH TO THE JORDAN RIVER

Life as Individuals

The Lord had given military victories to the chosen people. He had turned the curses of a false prophet into blessings for Israel. Yet the Lord also permits us a glimpse of his care for individuals as well as for the nation as a whole. In one situation several women were properly concerned about their inheritance and God shared their concern. In the other Moses was concerned about passing on the leadership role. In each case the Lord gave specific directives.

Zelophehad's Daughters

27 The daughters of Zelophehad son of Hepher, the son of Gilead, the son of Makir, the son of Manasseh, belonged to the clans of Manasseh son of Joseph. The names of the daughters were Mahlah, Noah, Hoglah, Milcah and Tirzah. They approached ²the entrance to the Tent of Meeting and stood before Moses, Eleazar the priest, the leaders and the whole assembly, and said, ³"Our father died in the desert. He was not among Korah's followers, who banded together against the LORD, but he died for his own sin and left no sons. ⁴Why should our father's name disappear from his clan because he had no son? Give us property among our father's relatives."

⁵So Moses brought their case before the LORD ⁶and the LORD said to him, ⁷"What Zelophehad's daughters are saying is right. You must certainly give them property as an inheritance among their father's relatives and turn their father's inheritance over to them.

⁸"Say to the Israelites, 'If a man dies and leaves no son, turn his inheritance over to his daughter. ⁹If he has no daughter, give his

inheritance to his brothers. [10]If he has no brothers, give his inheritance to his father's brothers. [11]If his father had no brothers, give his inheritance to the nearest relative in his clan, that he may possess it. This is to be a legal requirement for the Israelites, as the LORD commanded Moses.' "

The background for this incident involved the laws regarding inheritance. Property would normally be passed on to a male heir. Consequently the family described in this chapter had a real problem.

The circumstances were very simple and direct. The Lord had not blessed Zelophehad with a son. At this particular moment in the history of Israel that fact had great significance. The census had been designed to prepare for taking possession of the land of Canaan. Incidentally, it showed that the family of Zelophehad would be left out of the distribution of the land. There was no male heir in the family to whom the land could be assigned. In a most respectful and laudable way the daughters of Zelophehad presented their problem before the leaders of Israel. Since there were no guidelines for such a case, Moses brought the matter before the Lord.

The Lord acknowledged that the claim of the daughters was reasonable. Consequently in simple fairness Zelophehad, even though he was dead, was assigned a portion among his brethren. That portion was to be divided among the daughters. The Lord did not want these women to be disinherited. They too were to have a portion among the people.

The Lord also used this occasion to make a general ordinance. It was designed to keep the inheritance of land in the family and tribe to which it had originally been assigned. The net result of the ordinance was that the land should remain first of all in the family, but if there is no family, then it is to remain with the nearest relative in the clan. This was to be an ongoing ordinance for the children of Israel.

Joshua to Succeed Moses

12Then the LORD said to Moses, "Go up this mountain in the Abarim range and see the land I have given the Israelites. 13After you have seen it, you too will be gathered to your people, as your brother Aaron was, 14for when the community rebelled at the waters in the Desert of Zin, both of you disobeyed my command to honor me as holy before their eyes." (These were the waters of Meribah Kadesh, in the Desert of Zin.)

15Moses said to the LORD, 16"May the LORD, the God of the spirits of all mankind, appoint a man over this community 17to go out and come in before them, one who will lead them out and bring them in, so the LORD's people will not be like sheep without a shepherd."

18So the LORD said to Moses, "Take Joshua son of Nun, a man in whom is the spirit, and lay your hand on him. 19Have him stand before Eleazar the priest and the entire assembly and commission him in their presence. 20Give him some of your authority so the whole Israelite community will obey him. 21He is to stand before Eleazar the priest, who will obtain decisions for him by inquiring of the Urim before the LORD. At his command he and the entire community of the Israelites will go out, and at his command they will come in."

22Moses did as the LORD commanded him. He took Joshua and had him stand before Eleazar the priest and the whole assembly. 23Then he laid his hands on him and commissioned him, as the LORD instructed through Moses.

As the time drew closer for the Israelites to enter the Promised Land, the day of Moses' death drew nearer. And so the Lord directed Moses to go up on the mountaintop and view the land of Canaan. Even though Moses would not be allowed to enter the land, the Lord still granted him the privilege of viewing it.

Moses showed again that he was first and foremost a faithful leader of the children of Israel. He did not object that it was time for him to die. Nor did he complain because the Lord had acted in judgment toward him and Aaron because they had sinned at Meribah. His concern was instead for the people of Israel. If the Lord were to take him away, the children of Israel should not be without a leader. Moses chose to bring this to the attention of the Lord.

The Lord declared that Joshua was to be the next leader. Joshua already had a measure of the Spirit of God which had been poured out when the seventy elders had been selected (Numbers 11:24f). What was yet to be done was to designate Joshua a leader through an appropriate ceremony. Then the people would acknowledge him as leader.

It had been unique that the prophetic, priestly and kingly office were all combined in Moses. Now only the kingly responsibilities would be transferred to Joshua. Joshua would not have the privilege of speaking directly with God, as Moses had. Instead, to determine the Lord's will, Joshua was to consult with the priest, who would use the Urim (which was a part of the high priest's equipment). By consulting the Urim the high priest would be able to give Joshua directions from the Lord. Although his calling was not identical to Moses's calling, part of Moses' authority was conferred upon Joshua. His commissioning was public so that the people could see it. Then Joshua was to be given divine authority so that the people would become accustomed to following him. All this was designed so the people would go out and come in under the order of Joshua.

In this way the torch of national leadership was passed!

(At this point it should be noted that additional accounts of the commissioning of Joshua are given in Deuteronomy 31:7; 31:14ff; 34:9. Those accounts seem to refer back to this historical account and give us additional details from the memory of Moses.)

PART IV
PREPARATIONS AT THE JORDAN

NUMBERS 28—36

The fourth part of the book of Numbers is devoted to the time that the children of Israel spent encamped on the east bank of the Jordan River. In this section the Lord addressed the final phases of the preparation before the nation would move into the Promised Land.

The specific materials deal with the worship life. There is a summary of all the offerings and festivals and more directives about vows. The Israelites were directed to move out in vengeance against the Midianites. The life of the community focuses more and more on the imminent entry into the Promised Land. Several tribes preferred to settle east of the Jordan; there is a flashback to earlier stages of the journey that was now coming to an end; because the promise of the Lord is sure, the people could even note the boundaries and the towns. For the protection of individuals the Lord anticipated the need for cities of refuge and also dealt with another issue for the daughters of Zelophehad.

Life in Worship

As the children of Israel were about to enter the Promised Land the Lord reviewed all the sacrifices the people were to bring and festivals they were to observe. There were some adjustments that reflected the fact that the people would be scattered instead of living in a camp. But far more important was the overview of the annual outline of worship. The other aspect of worship that is addressed is the matter of vows. More directives deal with the limits that are placed on vows in the family situation.

Daily Offerings

28 **The LORD said to Moses, ²"Give this command to the Israelites and say to them: 'See that you present to me at the appointed time the food for my offerings made by fire, as an aroma pleasing to me.' ³Say to them: 'This is the offering made by fire that you are to present to the LORD: two lambs a year old without defect, as a regular burnt offering each day. ⁴Prepare one lamb in the morning and the other at twilight, ⁵together with a grain offering of a tenth of an ephah of fine flour mixed with a quarter of a hin of oil from pressed olives. ⁶This is the regular burnt offering instituted at Mount Sinai as a pleasing aroma, an offering made to the LORD by fire. ⁷The accompanying drink offering is to be a quarter of a hin of fermented drink with each lamb. Pour out the drink offering to the LORD at the sanctuary. ⁸Prepare the second lamb at twilight, along with the same kind of grain offering and drink offering that you prepare in the morning. This is an offering made by fire, an aroma pleasing to the LORD.' "**

In chapters 28-29 the Lord instructed Moses to record an overview and summary of the scheduled offerings that were to be brought by the Israelites. The list begins with the most regular sacrifice, the morning and evening offerings. The specific offering was a spotless lamb together with the accompanying grain and a drink offering.

Through this daily offering the Lord wanted to keep several important truths before the eyes of the people. One basic truth that underlay all of the blood sacrifices was the fact that death was necessary to atone for sin. God made it very clear that blood was the vehicle of atonement. "Without the shedding of blood there is no forgiveness" (Hebrews 9:22). Yet the sacrifice of lambs could not in itself atone for sin, so the sacrifice had to be repeated daily. Indeed, each sacrifice was really looking forward to the Lamb of God, the Lamb without blemish and without spot, the Messiah. He alone was the One who could forever atone for sins through his sin-offering on the cross. To that Lamb of God each lamb that was offered in a daily procession of morning and evening offerings looked forward.

The other truth taught by the morning and evening sacrifice can be seen from the fact that the sacrifice, known as the burnt offering, was a holocaust. In the other three blood sacrifices only portions of the animal victim were consumed by fire. In the case of the burnt offering, the entire sacrificial victim went up in smoke. As such it symbolized the worshiper's total dedication to God (see Romans 12:1).

Sabbath Offerings

9" 'On the Sabbath day, make an offering of two lambs a year old without defect, together with its drink offering and a grain offering of two-tenths of an ephah of fine flour mixed with oil. 10This is the burnt offering for every Sabbath, in addition to the regular burnt offering and its drink offering.' "

The next most regular offering was the Sabbath offering. Every seventh day the people were to bring an additional offering in the Tent of Meeting. This commemorated the fact that the Lord had rested on the seventh day and looked forward to the rest that God would give in his Messiah. The symbolism was the same since two lambs were sacrificed in addition to the regular, daily morning and evening offering.

Monthly Offerings

[11]" 'On the first of every month, present to the LORD a burnt offering of two young bulls, one ram and seven male lambs a year old, all without defect. [12]With each bull there is to be a grain offering of three-tenths of an ephah of fine flour mixed with oil, with the ram, a grain offering of two-tenths of an ephah of fine flour mixed with oil [13]and with each lamb, a grain offering of a tenth of an ephah of fine flour mixed with oil. This is for a burnt offering, a pleasing aroma, an offering made to the LORD by fire. [14]With each bull there is to be a drink offering of half a hin of wine; with the ram a third of a hin; and with each lamb, a quarter of a hin. This is the monthly burnt offering to be made at each new moon during the year. [15]Besides the regular burnt offering with its drink offering, one male goat is to be presented to the LORD as a sin offering.' "

Each month the time of new moon was marked by additional sacrifices. Besides the daily burnt offerings the people were to offer two bulls, one ram and seven male lambs. These offerings were to mark the fact that God had been gracious to the nation over the longer cycle as the moon increased and decreased.

The Passover

[16]" 'On the fourteenth day of the first month the LORD's Passover is to be held. [17]On the fifteenth day of this month there is to be a festival; for seven days eat bread made without yeast. [18]On the first day hold a sacred assembly and do no regular work. [19]Present to the LORD an offering made by fire, a burnt offering of two young bulls, one ram and seven male lambs a year old, all without defect. [20]With each bull prepare a grain offering of three-tenths of an ephah of fine flour mixed with oil; with the ram, two-tenths; [21]and with each of the seven lambs, one-tenth. [22]Include one male goat as a sin offering to make atonement for you. [23]Prepare these in addition to the regular morning burnt offering.

206

²⁴In this way prepare the food for the offering made by fire every day for seven days as an aroma pleasing to the LORD; it is to be prepared in addition to the regular burnt offering and its drink offering. ²⁵On the seventh day hold a sacred assembly and do no regular work.' "

The Passover was the first of the annual festivals which the children of Israel were to observe. Indeed, the whole religious calendar was based on the deliverance from Egypt. Each spring, just after the full moon following the spring equinox, the people through the Passover festival were to look back to the moment when the Lord graciously delivered them from slavery in Egypt. Everyone was to become involved by eating unleavened bread, by attending the solemn assembly and by doing no work either on the first day or on the last day of the festival. The rituals and sacrifices of the Passover were to be in addition to the regular daily sacrifices. The Passover sacrifices were also to be in addition to the preparations and celebration that was to take place in each home. The prescribed sacrifices were to be on behalf of the entire nation and so commemorated the protection of the firstborn from death, the deliverance from Egypt and the birth of the nation.

In a similar way in the New Testament we focus in spring on the Easter festival. Because our Savior has risen as victor over sin, Satan and death, we can celebrate our deliverance from the unholy three. As a celebration of deliverance from death both the Old and New Testament festivals provide some parallel thoughts, even though the rituals are not identical.

Feast of Weeks

²⁶" 'On the day of firstfruits, when you present to the LORD an offering of new grain during the Feast of Weeks, hold a sacred

assembly and do no regular work. ^{27} Present a burnt offering of two young bulls, one ram and seven male lambs a year old as an aroma pleasing to the Lord. ^{28} With each bull there is to be a grain offering of three-tenths of an ephah of fine flour mixed with oil; with the ram, two-tenths; ^{29} and with each of the seven lambs, one-tenth. ^{30} Include one male goat to make atonement for you. ^{31} Prepare these together with their drink offerings, in addition to the regular burnt offering and its grain offering. Be sure the animals are without defect.' "

The Feast of Weeks, Israel's spring harvest festival, bears striking similarity to the Christian Pentecost festival. Just as Pentecost is fifty days after Easter, so the Feast of Weeks was celebrated fifty days after the Passover. The number seven is noteworthy again and the Feast of Weeks represents seven sevens (weeks).

Again generous offerings were to be brought to the Lord and a special celebration was to be observed. The special feature of the Feast of Weeks was the offering of firstfruits. Those offerings came from the annual grain harvest. Therefore this festival was a very joyous occasion, filled with thoughts of thanksgiving.

When the Lord chose to send his Holy Spirit on the New Testament church at Pentecost, the firstfruits of the harvest of souls appeared. When the apostles were able to speak in many languages they set into motion a harvest that spread over the face of the whole world.

Feast of Trumpets

29 " 'On the first day of the seventh month hold a sacred assembly and do no regular work. It is a day for you to sound the trumpets. ^{2} As an aroma pleasing to the Lord, prepare a burnt offering of one young bull, one ram and seven male lambs a year old, all without defect. ^{3} With the bull prepare a grain offering of three-tenths of an ephah of fine flour mixed with oil; with the ram, two-tenths; ⁴and with each of the seven lambs, one-tenth. ⁵Include one male goat as a sin offering to make atonement for you. ⁶These are in addition to the monthly and daily burnt offerings with their grain offerings and drink offerings as specified. They are offerings made to the LORD by fire — a pleasing aroma.' "

The seventh month was a busy month for the Israelite worshiper. In addition to the daily sacrifices and the Sabbath celebrations, there were three festivals: the Feast of Trumpets on the first day of the month; the Day of Atonement on the tenth; and the Feast of Tabernacles, the fall harvest festival, from the fifteenth to the twenty-second.

Even as the joy was expressed by the trumpets, there was the constant reminder for the Israelites that we all receive our gifts from the Lord, purely out of his divine goodness and mercy. All people still had to come before him with sacrifices for sin. Indeed, there was to be quite a combination of sacrifices, since the daily sacrifices, the monthly sacrifices and the special sacrifices of this festival were to be brought before the Lord on this one particular day.

Day of Atonement

⁷" 'On the tenth day of this seventh month hold a sacred assembly. You must deny yourselves and do no work. ⁸Present as an aroma pleasing to the LORD a burnt offering of one young bull, one ram and seven male lambs a year old, all without defect. ⁹With the bull prepare a grain offering of three-tenths of an ephah of fine flour mixed with oil; with the ram, two-tenths; ¹⁰and with each of the seven lambs, one-tenth. ¹¹Include one male goat as a sin offering, in addition to the sin offering for atonement and the regular burnt offering with its grain offering, and their drink offerings.' "

The Day of Atonement was the Good Friday of the Old Testament. In solemn ritual special sin offerings were sacrificed and the blood sprinkled on the atonement cover in the Most Holy Place. The high priest was then to lay his hands on the head of the so-called scapegoat. This act symbolized that the high priest, acting on behalf of all the people, was laying the sins of the people on the goat. Then the goat would be led out of the camp and released, symbolizing the way the LORD was putting away the sins of the people.

All of this reminds us New Testament Christians that Jesus became our "scapegoat" who was taken outside of Jerusalem and paid for our sins on Calvary. The Day of Atonement was the only day of the year when the high priest would enter into the Most Holy Place and sprinkle blood on the atonement cover. Through this action God was once more teaching his people that blood was necessary to atone for the sins of the people.

Feast of Tabernacles

12" **'On the fifteenth day of the seventh month, hold a sacred assembly and do no regular work. Celebrate a festival to the LORD for seven days. **13**Present an offering made by fire as an aroma pleasing to the LORD, a burnt offering of thirteen young bulls, two rams and fourteen male lambs a year old, all without defect. **14**With each of the bulls prepare a grain offering of three-tenths of an ephah of fine flour mixed with oil; with each of the two rams, two-tenths; **15**and with each of the fourteen lambs, one-tenth. **16**Include one male goat as a sin offering, in addition to the regular burnt offering with its grain offering and drink offering.**

17" **'On the second day prepare twelve young bulls, two rams and fourteen male lambs a year old, all without defect. **18**With the bulls, rams and lambs, prepare their grain offerings and drink offerings according to the number specified. **19**Include one male goat as a sin offering, in addition to the regular burnt offering with its grain offering, and their drink offerings.**

²⁰" 'On the third day prepare eleven bulls, two rams and four-teen male lambs a year old, all without defect. ²¹With the bulls, rams and lambs, prepare their grain offerings and drink offerings according to the number specified. ²²Include one male goat as a sin offering, in addition to the regular burnt offering with its grain offering and drink offering.

²³" 'On the fourth day prepare ten bulls, two rams and fourteen male lambs a year old, all without defect. ²⁴With the bulls, rams and lambs, prepare their grain offerings and drink offerings according to the number specified. ²⁵Include one male goat as a sin offering, in addition to the regular burnt offering with its grain offering and drink offering.

²⁶" 'On the fifth day prepare nine bulls, two rams and fourteen male lambs a year old, all without defect. ²⁷With the bulls, rams and lambs, prepare their grain offerings and drink offerings according to the number specified. ²⁸Include one male goat as a sin offering, in addition to the regular burnt offering with its grain offering and drink offering.

²⁹" 'On the sixth day prepare eight bulls, two rams and fourteen male lambs a year old, all without defect. ³⁰With the bulls, rams and lambs, prepare their grain offerings and drink offerings according to the number specified. ³¹Include one male goat as a sin offering, in addition to the regular burnt offering with its grain offering and drink offering.

³²" 'On the seventh day prepare seven bulls, two rams and fourteen male lambs a year old, all without defect. ³³With the bulls, rams and lambs, prepare their grain offerings and drink offerings according to the number specified. ³⁴Include one male goat as a sin offering, in addition to the regular burnt offering with its grain offering and drink offering.

³⁵" 'On the eighth day hold an assembly and do no regular work. ³⁶Present an offering made by fire as an aroma pleasing to the LORD, a burnt offering of one bull, one ram and seven male lambs a year old, all without defect. ³⁷With the bull, the ram and the lambs, prepare their grain offerings and drink offerings according to the number specified. ³⁸Include one male goat as a sin

offering, in addition to the regular burnt offering with its grain offering and drink offering.

[39] " 'In addition to what you vow and your freewill offerings, prepare these for the LORD at your appointed feasts: your burnt offerings, grain offerings, drink offerings and fellowship offerings.' "

[40] Moses told the Israelites all that the LORD commanded him.

What a climax of thanksgiving! In the Feast of Tabernacles rich and generous offerings were sacrificed to the LORD. Although there would be a decreasing number of offerings on each of the seven days of the festival, the total is remarkable.

When the people had completed the fruit harvest in the fall each year, they were to join in a grand celebration that pointed to the fact that all blessings were indeed from the God of all mercy and grace.

In reviewing the sacrifices and festivals it is evident that the festivals occur in a span of seven lunar months — from the first month to the seventh month. In this way the Israelites had a festival half of the year for their worship life. In the same way the Christian church year celebrates a series of festivals from Advent through Pentecost. This is known as the festival half of the church year. In it we do just as the Israelites did — we review for adults and teach little children the wonderful things God has done for us. The balance of the church year focuses on encouraging us to faithfully serve the Lord who is so gracious to us.

Another interesting observation about the worship life of the Israelites is the frequency with which the number seven occurs. They had a sabbath of days, which ended with the sabbath each Saturday. (The Hebrew term "sabbath" means both "seven" and "rest.") They had a sabbath of weeks, the seven weeks between the Passover and the

Feast of Firstfruits. They had a sabbath of months as the seventh month contained a series of special festivals, including the great Day of Atonement. They also had a sabbath of years, in which they were to especially mark each seventh year. And every fifty years they had a sabbath of sabbatical years, which was known as the Jubilee year. In that year every debt was to be forgiven and property was to be returned to the original owner. All of these combinations of sevens point forward to the rest that remains for the people of God (Hebrews 4:9). When we have finished our course on earth, the Lord will be calling us into the eternal rest of heaven. In that rest all the other sabbaths reach their final purpose and goal.

Vows

30 **Moses said to the heads of the tribes of Israel: "This is what the LORD commands: ²When a man makes a vow to the LORD or takes an oath to obligate himself by a pledge, he must not break his word but must do everything he said.**

³"When a young woman still living in her father's house makes a vow to the LORD or obligates herself by a pledge ⁴and her father hears about her vow or pledge but says nothing to her, then all her vows and every pledge by which she obligated herself will stand. ⁵But if her father forbids her when he hears about it, none of her vows or the pledges by which she obligated herself will stand; the LORD will release her because her father has forbidden her.

⁶"If she marries after she makes a vow or after her lips utter a rash promise by which she obligates herself ⁷and her husband hears about it but says nothing to her, then her vows or the pledges by which she obligated herself will stand. ⁸But if her husband forbids her when he hears about it, he nullifies the vow that obligates her or the rash promise by which she obligates herself, and the LORD will release her.

⁹"Any vow or obligation taken by a widow or divorced woman will be binding on her.

¹⁰"If a woman living with her husband makes a vow or obligates herself by a pledge under oath ¹¹and her husband hears about it but says nothing to her and does not forbid her, then all her vows or the pledges by which she obligated herself will stand. ¹²But if her husband nullifies them when he hears about them, then none of the vows or pledges that came from her lips will stand. Her husband has nullified them, and the LORD will release her. ¹³Her husband may confirm or nullify any vow she makes or any sworn pledge to deny herself. ¹⁴But if her husband says nothing to her about it from day to day, then he confirms all her vows or the pledges binding on her. He confirms them by saying nothing to her when he hears about them. ¹⁵If, however, he nullifies them some time after he hears about them, then he is responsible for her guilt."

¹⁶These are the regulations the LORD gave Moses concerning relationships between a man and his wife, and between a father and his young daughter still living in his house.

At the command of the Lord Moses once again addresses the matter of voluntary vows. In such vows a person would take upon himself a certain discipline or purpose through which he wanted to serve the Lord. Such vows were voluntary. They would be in addition to any of the regulations and directions that were part of the Lord's ordinances for all the children of Israel.

The first principle presented here was that anyone who undertook a vow to the Lord was to carry out the vow in all seriousness. He didn't have to make a vow to the Lord, but if he did he had to keep it; there was no turning back. The person had to follow through on anything and everything that he had promised. This principle applied to the head of a household without reservation. In this chapter the head of a household included either the man of a household or a widowed or divorced woman who was in charge of a household.

But the Lord also knew that sinful human nature loves to pit one authority against another. Thus it could happen that someone who was not the head of the household would make a vow. In the enthusiasm of the moment the person would go beyond what was prudent and appropriate for that household. In this circumstance the Lord clearly underscored his will that the head of the household should really act as head of the household. Therefore the vows of those who were in a subordinate role in the home were always dependent on the acceptance of the vow by the head of the household. So the vows of children, young women and married women were contingent upon the approval of the head of the household. On the other hand, lest the head would foul things up by indecision, the mere fact that he said nothing would validate the vow.

When the head of the household heard about the vow, he had the right to make an immediate decision. If he approved the vow or at least if he did not object to the vow, the vow of the subordinate person would stand. The decision had to be made the first time that the head of the household heard about the vow. Therefore if as the head of the household he felt that the vow was inappropriate in his home, he could nullify it. The Lord indicated his willingness to accept the decision of the head of the household and proclaimed that there would be no guilt. On the other hand, the head of the household could not vacillate later. He could not change his mind later on. If the person did not immediately make the decision to nullify the vow the first time it was heard, the vow was validated. Once the vow had been validated there was no turning back. The person who had made the vow would have to follow through till the vow was discharged.

In this way the Lord headed off possible conflicts that could arise as the subordinated persons would say that they had vowed to the Lord and therefore the head of the household could not stop them. By pitting two superiors against each other confusion could have resulted. But the Lord here shows just how serious he is about supporting the head of the household. He specifically gives the head of the household the right to overrule even the gifts that were promised to God by members of his household.

How carefully the divine directives provide for good order in families. How clearly he preserves the power of superiors and defines the duty and reverence due from those under authority! Rather than break these bonds, God lays aside his right and releases the obligation of a solemn vow.

PREPARATIONS AT THE JORDAN

Life While Moving Out

The Lord had brought the Israelites to the edge of the Promised Land. There were not many more stages to the journey, but there was some unfinished business. Therefore the Lord directed the people to attack the Midianites. The reason was because the Israelites were to be the agents of God's vengeance against a people who had purposely led the Israelites into idolatry. Several remarkable things happened. The hand of the Lord gave a victory so complete that no Israelite was killed in the battle. The Lord also moved the hearts of the people to bring a large part of the spoil as a offering to the Lord.

Vengeance on the Midianites

31 The LORD said to Moses, [2]"Take vengeance on the Midianites for the Israelites. After that, you will be gathered to your people."

[3]So Moses said to the people, "Arm some of your men to go to war against the Midianites and to carry out the LORD's vengeance on them. [4]Send into battle a thousand men from each of the tribes of Israel." [5]So twelve thousand men armed for battle, a thousand from each tribe, were supplied from the clans of Israel. [6]Moses sent them into battle, a thousand from each tribe, along with Phinehas son of Eleazar, the priest, who took with him articles from the sanctuary and the trumpets for signaling.

[7]They fought against Midian, as the LORD commanded Moses, and killed every man. [8]Among their victims were Evi, Rekem, Zur, Hur and Reba — the five kings of Midian. They also killed

Balaam son of Beor with the sword. ⁹The Israelites captured the Midianite women and children and took all the Midianite herds, flocks and goods as plunder. ¹⁰They burned all the towns where the Midianites had settled, as well as all their camps. ¹¹They took all the plunder and spoils, including the people and animals, ¹²and brought the captives, spoils and plunder to Moses and Eleazar the priest and the Israelite assembly at their camp on the plains of Moab, by the Jordan across from Jericho.

¹³Moses, Eleazar the priest and all the leaders of the community went to meet them outside the camp. ¹⁴Moses was angry with the officers of the army — the commanders of thousands and commanders of hundreds — who returned from the battle.

¹⁵"Have you allowed all the women to live?" he asked them. ¹⁶"They were the ones who followed Balaam's advice and were the means of turning the Israelites away from the Lord in what happened at Peor, so that a plague struck the Lord's people. ¹⁷Now kill all the boys. And kill every woman who has slept with a man, ¹⁸but save for yourselves every girl who has never slept with a man."

It has been said, "The mills of God grind slowly, but they grind exceedingly fine." The Midianites learned this the hard way as the Lord took action against them for their sinfulness described in chapter 25. At that time the Midianites, on the advice of Balaam, had led the Israelites into their idolatrous and adulterous worship practices (Numbers 25:1-18). The Lord had decreed a stern punishment; 24,000 Israelites were executed at that time by the judges. The punishment reached its climax when the priest Phinehas put a spear through the man who brought a Midianite woman to his tent. At the end of chapter 25 there is a note that the Lord had to take vengeance on the Midianite nation. Now was the time.

He directed Moses to command the people to attack them. (The Lord also added that following this attack,

Moses should be ready to die — to be gathered to his people.) The details of organizing the attack were apparently left to Moses.

He assembled an army composed of 1,000 men from each of the twelve tribes. This fighting unit of 12,000 men was to be the instrument of God's vengeance. It is noted that Phinehas the priest went with the army, carrying unnamed instruments from the tabernacle. The priest also took the trumpets that would be used to give the soldiers orders both on the march and in battle.

The Israelites gained total victory and killed all the men. Among the victims were five kings of the Midianites. It is especially noteworthy that Balaam, the prophet who tried unsuccessfully to curse Israel, was among the victims. Apparently after Balaam left Balak without cursing Israel, he had returned to his home. Soon after he must have returned to the Midianites. How sad that his prayer that he might die like the Israelites (23:10) was not realized! He had been so close, but had apparently turned back completely to his soothsaying and gave the advice that led the children of Israel into the adulterous and idolatrous worship.

The cities and camps of the Midianites were totally destroyed. The women and children were taken captive. The animals were the booty of war. Bringing the people and animals with them, the army returned to the Israelite camp. Naturally they were pleased with themselves.

But Moses was angry! When he saw that the Midianite women had been saved, he spoke in righteous anger. He rightly pointed out that it was these women who had misled the Israelites. They were the ones who had invited the men to engage in the adulterous worship of Baal, the Canaanite fertility god. So Moses ordered that all the boys and all the women who had slept with a man were to be put to death.

The men of the army carried out this stern judgment from the Lord. So this clan of the Midianites was effectively exterminated.

It is interesting to note that Moses seemed to know that Balaam had been the instigator who worked behind the scenes. He puts the full blame for the temptation that led to Israel's apostasy and to the destruction of the Midianites on Balaam, the compromising soothsayer.

At first it may seem strange that Moses and Eleazar met the army outside of the camp. But because battles involve death the men of the army were ceremonially unclean. Therefore Moses and Eleazar reminded them of their responsibilities to reestablish their ceremonial cleanness before they entered the camp.

Purification from Uncleanness

[19]"All of you who have killed anyone or touched anyone who was killed must stay outside the camp seven days. On the third and seventh days you must purify yourselves and your captives. [20]Purify every garment as well as everything made of leather, goat hair or wood."

[21]Then Eleazar the priest said to the soldiers who had gone into battle, "This is the requirement of the law that the LORD gave Moses: [22]Gold, silver, bronze, iron, tin, lead [23]and anything else that can withstand fire must be put through the fire, and then it will be clean. But it must also be purified with the water of cleansing. And whatever cannot withstand fire must be put through that water. [24]On the seventh day wash your clothes and you will be clean. Then you may come into the camp."

In chapter 19 Moses had presented the ordinances regarding the ceremonial uncleanness of anyone who had been in contact with a dead person. It's likely that most people in this army of 12,000 had either killed someone or touched some corpse. They therefore had to follow the ritual for ceremonial purification both for themselves and for the captives they had taken. On the third and seventh day they had to use the water of cleansing.

The main new information in these paragraphs was that items made of leather, goat hair, wood or metal were also to be purified. Anything that could be passed through fire without being destroyed was to be purified by fire. Later it also had to be purified with the water of cleansing. Items that could not be passed through fire were to be cleansed with the waters of cleansing. Clothes had to be washed on the seventh day. Then after bathing the people would be ceremonially clean. Only then could they return to the camp.

Dividing the Spoils

25The LORD said to Moses, 26"You and Eleazar the priest and the family heads of the community are to count all the people and animals that were captured. 27Divide the spoils between the soldiers who took part in the battle and the rest of the community. 28From the soldiers who fought in the battle, set apart as tribute for the LORD one out of every five hundred, whether persons, cattle, donkeys, sheep or goats. 29Take this tribute from their half share and give it to Eleazar the priest as the LORD's part. 30From the Israelites' half, select one out of every fifty, whether persons, cattle, donkeys, sheep, goats or other animals. Give them to the Levites, who are responsible for the care of the LORD's tabernacle." 31So Moses and Eleazar the priest did as the LORD commanded Moses.

32The plunder remaining from the spoils that the soldiers took was 675,000 sheep, 3372,000 cattle, 3461,000 donkeys 35and 32,000 women who had never slept with a man.

36The half share of those who fought in the battle was:

337,500 sheep, 37of which the tribute for the LORD was 675;
3836,000 cattle, of which the tribute for the LORD was 72;

221

[39] 30,500 donkeys, of which the tribute for the LORD was 61;

[40] 16,000 people, of which the tribute for the LORD was 32;

[41] Moses gave the tribute to Eleazar the priest as the LORD's part, as the LORD commanded Moses.

[42] The half belonging to the Israelites, which Moses set apart from that of the fighting men — [43] the community's half — was 337,500 sheep, [44] 36,000 cattle, [45] 30,500 donkeys [46] and 16,000 people. [47] From the Israelites' half, Moses selected one out of every fifty persons and animals, as the LORD commanded him, and gave them to the Levites, who were responsible for the care of the LORD's tabernacle.

The Lord decreed that the spoils were to be divided into halves. One half went to the soldiers who had actually done the fighting. The other half would be assigned to the people of the entire nation. But even in dividing booty the Lord's share was not to be forgotten. In this case the Lord was to receive one-fifth of one percent of the booty that the soldiers received and two percent of the booty that the people in general received. The part for the Lord from the soldiers' portion was to be given to the high priest, and the part from the people in general was to go to the Levites.

In examining the numbers it becomes obvious that the booty was a very sizable addition to the riches of the Israelites.

A Special Thank Offering

[48] Then the officers who were over the units of the army — the commanders of thousands and commanders of hundreds — went to Moses [49] and said to him, "Your servants have counted the soldiers under our command, and not one is missing. [50] So we have brought as an offering to the LORD the gold articles each of us acquired — armlets, bracelets, signet rings, earrings and necklaces — to make atonement for ourselves before the LORD."

[51]Moses and Eleazar the priest accepted from them the gold — all the crafted articles. [52]All the gold from the commanders of thousands and commanders of hundreds that Moses and Eleazar presented as a gift to the LORD weighed 16,750 shekels. [53]Each soldier had taken plunder for himself. [54]Moses and Eleazar the priest accepted the gold from the commanders of thousands and commanders of hundreds and brought it into the Tent of Meeting as a memorial for the Israelites before the LORD.

In the midst of the victory a most remarkable thing had happened! Although it appears the Israelite fighting force had been outnumbered, not a single Israelite soldier had been killed! Such a miraculous outcome even in a single battle would have been remarkable enough. The miracle was the more remarkable because the entire campaign had involved taking a number of cities and villages. The commanders of thousands and the commanders of hundreds had taken a careful count. Every one of their men had survived. The Lord had protected them all! Such a blessing was far greater than anything they had a right to expect. It was becoming more and more obvious that God could and would protect the children that the Israelites of the previous generation had thought would never be able to take the Promised Land. With a strong arm and on mighty wings the Lord was leading this people. Once again the words of Joshua and Caleb come to mind: "The LORD is with us."

For such an outstanding blessing the officers and soldiers wanted to express appreciation. Consequently the officers came to Moses and said that they would give up all the booty that was made of gold. Since the Lord had not required this booty in the previous instructions, each man really owned whatever he had found. However, they now offered it to the Lord as a thankoffering for his remarkable protection. In passing, Moses notes that the gold that was offered weighed about 420 pounds.

Through this victory over the Midianites the Lord put the finishing touches on establishing a safe area for the Israelites. The whole rectangle of land between the Jordan River in the west and the Arabian Desert in the east, between the Sea of Galilee in the north and the Salt Sea in the south was now secure. The Israelites no longer need fear harassment from the Midianities who normally wandered about on the edge of the desert east of the Jordan.

PREPARATIONS AT THE JORDAN

Life in the Community

In the final days a momentous decision by several Israelite tribes directly affected their future history. Those tribes were impressed by the geography of the land east of the Jordan. It was well suited for raising cattle. Since ranching was their preferred occupation they requested permission to settle in the land they had already conquered. After some negotiation, Moses gave them permission. The material that follows is a record of all the stages in the journey that the Israelites had made since their deliverance from Egypt. Such a review of God's guidance could only call forth the words of praise, "The LORD has been with us!"

Then, even though not a square inch of the land between the Jordan and the Mediterranean Sea had been captured, the Lord defined the boundaries of the land he was giving the children of Israel. To make his promises even more emphatic, the Lord also arranged that certain cities that were yet to be captured, were to be the towns of the Levites.

The Transjordan Tribes

32 **The Reubenites and Gadites, who had very large herds and flocks, saw that the lands of Jazer and Gilead were suitable for livestock. ²So they came to Moses and Eleazar the priest and to the leaders of the community, and said, ³"Ataroth, Dibon, Jazer, Nimrah, Heshbon, Elealeh, Sebam, Nebo and Beon — ⁴the land the LORD subdued before the people of Israel — are suitable for livestock, and your servants have livestock. ⁵If we have found favor in your eyes," they said, "let this land be given to your servants as our possession. Do not make us cross the Jordan."**

⁶Moses said to the Gadites and Reubenites, "Shall your countrymen go to war while you sit here? ⁷Why do you discourage the Israelites from going over into the land the LORD has given them? ⁸This is what your fathers did when I sent them from Kadesh Barnea to look over the land. ⁹After they went up to the Valley of Eshcol and viewed the land, they discouraged the Israelites from entering the land the LORD had given them. ¹⁰The LORD's anger was aroused that day and he swore this oath: ¹¹'Because they have not followed me wholeheartedly, not one of the men twenty years old or more who came up out of Egypt will see the land I promised on oath to Abraham, Isaac and Jacob —¹²not one except Caleb son of Jephunneh the Kenizzite and Joshua son of Nun, for they followed the LORD wholeheartedly,' ¹³The LORD's anger burned against Israel and he made them wander in the desert forty years, until the whole generation of those who had done evil in his sight was gone.

¹⁴"And here you are, a brood of sinners, standing in the place of your fathers and making the LORD even more angry with Israel. ¹⁵If you turn away from following him, he will again leave all this people in the desert, and you will be the cause of their destruction."

Under the Lord's blessing and direction the Israelites had already conquered a sizable portion of open country on the east side of the Jordan River. The area around Jazer and Gilead was cattle country. The long, sloping hills were better suited to grazing than to farming. In the eyes of the Reubenites and Gadites ranchland was exactly the type of land they wanted. Therefore they approached Moses with the request for permission to settle in this territory.

The reaction of Moses was almost vehement! He equated the desire of the Reubenites and Gadites with the rebelliousness of the people who had refused to go forward into Canaan forty years earlier. At first this may seem a pretty harsh judgment. Yet the proposal had ended with the words: "Do not make us cross the Jordan."

When we look at the request, we see it was indeed riddled with selfishness. Considering only their own desires and ignoring the bond of unity with the rest of the nation they wanted to settle down. At very least, wasn't it thoughtless of them to want the territories that the entire nation had conquered? Did they really intend to refuse to help the other tribes conquer a homeland for themselves? To Moses the request seemed very similar to the action of the previous generation when it refused to go forward into the Promised Land. Would their request discourage the other tribes? Would their decision deflect the rest of the nation from going into the land that God was giving them?

These possibilities were so overwhelming to Moses that he called the Reubenites and Gadites a brood of sinners. He also warned them lest they become the cause of further destruction of the people. If the Lord became angry and condemned the people to further wandering in the desert, it would be the fault of such a sinful, selfish, thoughtless group of people. How foolish to rebel against the Lord by choosing their own "promised land" — by being dissatisfied with the land that the Lord was about to give them!

Conquering Canaan to Be a Joint Effort

16Then they came up to him and said, "We would like to build pens here for our livestock and cities for our women and children. 17But we are ready to arm ourselves and go ahead of the Israelites until we have brought them to their place. Meanwhile our women and children will live in fortified cities, for protection from the inhabitants of the land. 18We will not return to our homes until every Israelite has received his inheritance. 19We will not receive any inheritance with them on the other side of the Jordan, because our inheritance has come to us on the east side of the Jordan."

227

²⁰Then Moses said to them, "If you will do this — if you will arm yourselves before the LORD for battle, ²¹and if all of you will go armed over the Jordan before the LORD until he has driven his enemies out before him — ²²then when the land is subdued before the LORD, you may return and be free from your obligation to the LORD and to Israel. And this land will be your possession before the LORD.

²³"But if you fail to do this, you will be sinning against the LORD; and you may be sure that your sin will find you out. ²⁴Build cities for your women and children, and pens for your flocks, but do what you have promised."

²⁵The Gadites and Reubenites said to Moses, "We your servants will do as our lord commands. ²⁶Our children and wives, our flocks and herds will remain here in the cities of Gilead. ²⁷But your servants, every man armed for battle, will cross over to fight before the LORD, just as our lord says."

²⁸Then Moses gave orders about them to Eleazar the priest and Joshua son of Nun and to the family heads of the Israelite tribes. ²⁹He said to them, "If the Gadites and Reubenites, every man armed for battle, cross over the Jordan with you before the LORD, then when the land is subdued before you, give them the land of Gilead as their possession. ³⁰But if they do not cross over with you armed, they must accept their possession with you in Canaan."

³¹The Gadites and Reubenites answered, "Your servants will do what the LORD has said. ³²We will cross over before the LORD into Canaan armed, but the property we inherit will be on this side of the Jordan."

³³Then Moses gave to the Gadites, the Reubenites and the half-tribe of Manasseh son of Joseph the kingdom of Sihon king of the Amorites and the kingdom of Og king of Bashan — the whole land with its cities and the territory around them.

It is not clear whether the Reubenites and Gadites had intended from the beginning to help in conquering the rest of the Promised Land. At any rate, they persisted with their request and offered to send their fighting men to go before the Israelites until all of Canaan had been conquered. By this promise they indicated that they in no way wanted to ignore or shirk any responsibilities they had toward the rest of the nation. In a practical sense, it was good for the Israelites to have a group of soldiers who would march before them who were not involved in moving a family and possessions.

When it became clear that the Reubenites and Gadites were ready to participate in conquering Canaan, Moses relented. He gave them permission to build the fortified areas they would need for their families and flocks. But he also laid on them the responsibility to follow through completely on their promises. If they failed to follow through on their promise, they would be denied permission to stay in Gilead and would have to live with the Israelites in an assigned inheritance on the west side of the Jordan.

The seriousness of their responsibility is made clear when Moses solemnly explained the arrangement to the high priest, to Joshua and to the heads of the various tribes. In the presence of that group of leaders the Reubenites and Gadites repeated their intention to send soldiers along to help in the conquest of the Promised Land. They did keep their promise. Their faithfulness was exemplary because later they were released from their promise after the land of Canaan had been conquered (Joshua 22:1-6).

So the negotiations came to an end. Somewhere near the end of the negotiations the half-tribe of Manasseh must also have asked to be included. Therefore the Reubenites, the Gadites and the half-tribe of Manasseh were allowed to make the necessary arrangements to settle in the area east of the Jordan.

The Settlements

³⁴The Gadites built up Dibon, Ataroth, Aroer, ³⁵Atroth Shophan, Jazer, Jogbehah, ³⁶Beth Nimrah and Beth Haran as fortified cities, and built pens for their flocks. ³⁷And the Reubenites rebuilt Heshbon, Elealeh and Kiriathaim, ³⁸as well as Nebo and Baal Meon (these names were changed) and Sibmah. They gave names to the cities they rebuilt.

³⁹The descendants of Makir son of Manasseh went to Gilead, captured it and drove out the Amorites who were there. ⁴⁰So Moses gave Gilead to the Makirites, the descendants of Manasseh, and they settled there. ⁴¹Jair, a descendant of Manasseh, captured their settlements and called them Havvoth Jair. ⁴²And Nobah captured Kenath and its surrounding settlements and called it Nobah after himself.

The geography of any particular place in the world tends to indicate that certain locations are the natural sites for cities. Consequently many of the cities that the transjordanian tribes rebuilt were at the same locations where cities had previously stood. In some cases the locations retained the same names that they previously had. For good reason other names were changed, especially those that referred to some pagan deity.

So everybody was happy. The transjordanian tribes had the type of land that suited their purposes, and the remaining tribes had the additional soldiers that would apparently be needed to conquer the Promised Land.

How well we also see the familiar rule that applies in the kingdom of God: first war and battle, then the inheritance. Those who will not fight the good fight should not expect an inheritance.

Stages in Israel's Journey

33 Here are the stages in the journey of the Israelites when they came out of Egypt by divisions under the leadership of

Moses and Aaron. ²At the LORD's command Moses recorded the stages in their journey. This is their journey by stages:

³The Israelites set out from Rameses on the fifteenth day of the first month, the day after the Passover. They marched out boldly in full view of all the Egyptians, ⁴who were burying all their firstborn, whom the LORD had struck down among them; for the LORD had brought judgment on their gods.

⁵The Israelites left Rameses and camped at Succoth.

⁶They left Succoth and camped at Etham, on the edge of the desert.

⁷They left Etham, turned back to Pi Hahiroth, to the east of Baal Zephon, and camped near Migdol.

⁸They left Pi Hahiroth and passed through the sea into the desert, and when they had traveled for three days in the Desert of Etham, they camped at Marah.

⁹They left Marah and went to Elim, where there were twelve springs and seventy palm trees, and they camped there.

¹⁰They left Elim and camped by the Red Sea.

¹¹They left the Red Sea and camped in the Desert of Sin.

¹²They left the Desert of Sin and camped at Dophkah.

¹³They left Dophkah and camped at Alush.

¹⁴They left Alush and camped at Rephidim, where there was no water for the people to drink.

¹⁵They left Rephidim and camped in the Desert of Sinai.

¹⁶They left the Desert of Sinai and camped at Kibroth Hattaavah.

¹⁷They left Kibroth Hattaavah and camped at Hazeroth.

¹⁸They left Hazeroth and camped at Rithmah.

¹⁹They left Rithmah and camped at Rimmon Perez.

²⁰They left Rimmon Perez and camped at Libnah.

²¹They left Libnah and camped at Rissah.

²²They left Rissah and camped at Kehelathah.

²³They left Kehelathah and camped at Mount Shepher.

²⁴They left Mount Shepher and camped at Haradah.

25They left Haradah and camped at Makheloth.

26They left Makheloth and camped at Tahath.

27They left Tahath and camped at Terah.

28They left Terah and camped at Mithcah.

29They left Mithcah and camped at Hashmonah.

30They left Hashmonah and camped at Moseroth.

31They left Moseroth and camped at Bene Jaakan.

32They left Bene Jaakan and camped at Hor Haggidgad.

33They left Hor Haggidgad and camped at Jotbathah.

34They left Jotbathah and camped at Abronah.

35They left Abronah and camped at Ezion Geber.

36They left Ezion Geber and camped at Kadesh, in the Desert of Zin.

37They left Kadesh and camped at Mount Hor, on the border of Edom. 38At the LORD's command Aaron the priest went up Mount Hor, where he died on the first day of the fifth month of the fortieth year after the Israelites came out of Egypt. 39Aaron was a hundred and twenty-three years old when he died on Mount Hor.

40The Canaanite king of Arad, who lived in the Negev of Canaan, heard that the Israelites were coming.

41They left Mount Hor and camped at Zalmonah.

42They left Zalmonah and camped at Punon.

43They left Punon and camped at Oboth.

44They left Oboth and camped at Iye Abarim, on the border of Moab.

45They left Iyim and camped at Dibon Gad.

46They left Dibon Gad and camped at Almon Diblathaim.

47They left Almon Diblathaim and camped in the mountains of Abarim, near Nebo.

48They left the mountains of Abarim and camped on the plains of Moab by the Jordan across from Jericho. 49There on the plains of Moab they camped along the Jordan from Beth Jeshimoth to Abel Shittim.

50On the plains of Moab by the Jordan across from Jericho the LORD said to Moses, 51"Speak to the Israelites and say to them:

'When you cross the Jordan into Canaan, [52]drive out all the inhabitants of the land before you. Destroy all their carved images and their cast idols, and demolish all their high places. [53]Take possession of the land and settle in it, for I have given you the land to possess. [54]Distribute the land by lot, according to your clans. To a larger group give a larger inheritance, and to a smaller group a smaller one. Whatever falls to them by lot will be theirs. Distribute it according to your ancestral tribes.

[55]'But if you do not drive out the inhabitants of the land, those you allow to remain will become barbs in your eyes and thorns in your sides. They will give you trouble in the land where you will live. [56]And then I will do to you what I plan to do to them.' "

In examining the list of campsites it soon becomes evident that this list provides the only information about some of the campsites. As was pointed out earlier, the Bible records a history of the spiritual life of the people of God, rather than a mechanical historical record. We must assume the Lord had determined that nothing significant happened that affected the spiritual direction of the Israelites at the sites where no additional information is given.

Earlier there was a broken record of the Israelites constant complaining against the Lord. It had started shortly after they left Sinai. The report about fire at the edge of the camp introduced such complaints. Just a brief note is made about that campsite, but it introduced a rising crescendo of complaint and rebellion which built to its climax in the revolt at Kadesh-barnea. In the same way there is a detailed description of the situation with the bronze serpent, but virtually nothing is said about the campsites where the Israelites stayed before and after that event. Here those events are simply placed into the context of a complete list of campsites.

The Lord's control of all events becomes clear in the precise timing of events. It is no coincidence that Aaron died in the fifth month of the fortieth year after the children of Israel came out of Egypt. Similarly the remaining events that are recorded after his death took place over those final months of the fortieth year. Thus the Israelites arrived at the Jordan precisely according to God's plan for them.

Since the Lord had commanded Moses to make a list of the campsites, he also used the occasion to repeat the instructions about the punishment he wanted to carry out on the Canaanites through the Israelites. Actually the Lord was using this nation as his tool to punish the Canaanites. Consequently their orders were to drive out and destroy all the Canaanites. Above all, they were to tear down and demolish the idol temples and the high places. Only by obeying this instruction from the Lord would they really be allowed to take possession of the land.

Since under God's blessing it was certain that the land would be conquered, it was perfectly logical to announce the general procedure for land distribution. Basically the plan provided that every individual would receive the same amount of land. From that it follows that the larger tribes would receive more land than the smaller tribes. Further, everything was to be determined by lot. Using lots obviously prevented the accusation of favoritism. The final assignment of land both for the tribes and for the individuals in the tribes was left to the Lord, the one who truly controls even lots.

The chapter closes with a solemn warning about the serious consequences that would follow if Israel failed to destroy the Canaanites or demolish their high places. Their assignment was: (1) to drive out the present inhabitants, and (2) to completely destroy all cult objects and sanctuaries that were used by the present inhabitants. If the Israelites allowed some of the Canaanites to stay in the land, those very people would become a serious problem. In the vivid language used here those people would become barbs in their eyes.

From our vantage point we know that the children of Israel did allow some Canaanites to survive. It was just those people (for example, the Philistines), who became a constant source of trouble for the Israelites in the centuries that followed.

God warned the Israelites that if they did not drive out the people of Canaan, they would bring down God's anger on themselves. He would carry out the same punishment upon them that they were to inflict on the Canaanites. How well the Lord remembers both his promises and his threats! When the Israelites were unfaithful they did indeed bring down God's anger on themselves and he did drive them from the land promised to their forefather Abraham. Yet the promises of grace in the Savior were all carried out before the Israelites were finally driven from the land. God's great purpose of providing salvation through a descendant of Abraham would and did certainly come to pass!

It is still the will of the Lord that Christians, although living in the midst of the godless children of this unbelieving world, should keep themselves uncontaminated by the world. Compromise with idolatry will inevitably lead to catastrophe.

Boundaries of Canaan

34 The LORD said to Moses, [2]"Command the Israelites and say to them: 'When you enter Canaan, the land that will be allotted to you as an inheritance will have these boundaries:

[3]" 'Your southern side will include some of the Desert of Zin along the border of Edom. On the east, your southern boundary will start from the end of the Salt Sea, [4]cross south of Scorpion Pass, continue on to Zin and go south of Kadesh Barnea. Then it

will go to Hazar Addar and over to Azmon, ⁵where it will turn, join the Wadi of Egypt and end at the Sea.

⁶" 'Your western boundary will be the coast of the Great Sea. This will be your boundary on the west.

⁷" 'For your northern boundary, run a line from the Great Sea to Mount Hor ⁸and from Mount Hor to Lebo Hamath. Then the boundary will go to Zedad, ⁹continue to Ziphron and end at Hazar Enan. This will be your boundary on the north.

¹⁰" 'For your eastern boundary, run a line from Hazar Enan to Shepham. ¹¹The boundary will go down from Shepham to Riblah on the east side of Ain and continue along the slopes east of the Sea of Kinnereth. ¹²Then the boundary will go down along the Jordan and end at the Salt Sea.

" 'This will be your land, with its boundaries on every side.' "

The territory that the Lord was giving the Israelites is roughly rectangular in shape. In looking at a map the lower right hand corner of the rectangle would be the south end of the Salt Sea (or, Dead Sea). A line drawn generally westward to the Great Sea (Mediterranean Sea) would be Israel's southern border. The Mediterranean itself would be the boundary on the west side. In the north the border would extend from the Great Sea to the top of the Sea of Kinnereth (Sea of Gennesaret or the Sea of Galilee). The border on the east would be the Jordan River. Outside of this rectangle would be Kadesh-barnea in the south, Lebo Hamath in the north (the location is uncertain) and the land of the two and one half tribes that settled east of the Jordan.

According to these directions, the Promised Land rests right on top of an isthmus of fertile land between the Arabian Desert and the Mediterranean Sea. The great caravans of trade that passed back and forth between Egypt and the empires along the Tigris and Euphrates Rivers had to pass through some part of this rectangle of land.

Consequently there was a cosmopolitan aspect to the land God chose as his people's homeland. There was also a trading atmosphere. The land also became the marching ground for many armies. Clearly the Lord's hand was over all. He used Canaan's strategic location as an opportunity to spread the gospel of the coming Messiah. Under his guidance his Word did spread far and wide. In the history that followed it is evident that when the children of Israel were faithful to the Lord, they prospered. On the other hand, when they were unfaithful the Lord sent armies to chastise them.

Assigning the Land

¹³Moses commanded the Israelites: "Assign this land by lot as an inheritance. The LORD has ordered that it be given to the nine and a half tribes, ¹⁴because the families of the tribe of Reuben, the tribe of Gad and the half-tribe of Manasseh have received their inheritance. ¹⁵These two and a half tribes have received their inheritance on the east side of the Jordan of Jericho, toward the sunrise."

¹⁶The LORD said to Moses, ¹⁷"These are the names of the men who are to assign the land for you as an inheritance: Eleazar the priest and Joshua son of Nun. ¹⁸And appoint one leader from each tribe to help assign the land. ¹⁹These are their names:

Caleb son of Jephunneh,
from the tribe of Judah;
²⁰Shemuel son of Ammihud,
from the tribe of Simeon;
²¹Elidad son of Kislon,
from the tribe of Benjamin;
²²Bukki son of Jogli,
the leader from the tribe of Dan;
²³Hanniel son of Ephod,
the leader from the tribe of Manasseh son of Joseph;
²⁴Kemuel son of Shiphtan,
the leader from the tribe of Ephraim son of Joseph;

237

²⁵Elizaphan son of Parnach,
    the leader from the tribe of Zebulun;
²⁶Paltiel son of Azzan,
    the leader from the tribe of Issachar;
²⁷Ahihud son of Shelomi,
    the leader from the tribe of Asher;
²⁸Pedahel son of Ammihud,
    the leader from the tribe of Naphtali."
²⁹These are the men the LORD commanded to assign the inheritance to the Israelites in the land of Canaan.

The procedure for assigning the land reflected procedures that had been used a number of times before. The political leader Joshua, the spiritual leader Eleazar, plus a leader from each of the twelve tribes were to act as officials. The list brings no special names except that of faithful Caleb, whom we have met on several previous occasions. That he was alive was significant because at Kadesh-barnea he and Joshua had been the ones who urged the people to go forward. On the basis of simple trust in the Lord they had said, "The LORD is with us." That faith was blessed at this point because Caleb was alive to help in the distribution of the land. He did take possession of his own land as the Lord had promised.

The people were to assign the territory by lot. In this way the Lord's hand would clearly direct all the aspects of the selection process. There would be no opportunity for jealousy. No one could complain about unfairness or favoritism. Each family could look at his inheritance as a gift from the Lord.

Isn't it fascinating to see the faith that is involved in all this activity? The land of Canaan had not yet been conquered. The many Canaanite tribes so vividly described by the spies forty years earlier still lived in the land. But God's people followed through on assigning the land because they acted in faith, knowing that what the Lord had promised he was fully able to do. That confidence is what distinguished this generation from the previous generation. They lived in the light of Caleb's words: "The LORD is with us."

Such is the confidence that the Lord wants to call forth from his people in every generation. Each promise of the Lord is sure of fulfillment. The divine realities are no different in our age. What God has promised, he will perform! He is fully capable of carrying out every one of his promises, whether it applies to the present or to the far distant future. In such confidence every Christian may conduct his life. In such confidence every Christian may face his death.

Towns for the Levites

35 On the plains of Moab by the Jordan across from Jericho, the LORD said to Moses, ²"Command the Israelites to give the Levites towns to live in from the inheritance the Israelites will possess. And give them pasturelands around the towns. ³Then they will have towns to live in and pasturelands for their cattle, flocks and all their other livestock.

⁴"The pasturelands around the towns that you give the Levites will extend out fifteen hundred feet from the town wall. ⁵Outside the town, measure three thousand feet on the east side, three thousand on the south side, three thousand on the west and three thousand on the north, with the town in the center. They will have this area as pastureland for the towns.

Originally the Lord had directed that all the firstborn of the Israelites would be dedicated to him. Under such an arrangement every family would have had someone who went to work at the Temple. As things worked out historically the Lord determined that the Levites would be the ones who would serve in the Tent of Meeting. But it was desirable that the information from the center of their religion should be sent out throughout the nation. Therefore

God determined that the Levites should be assigned cities throughout the whole land. They were to be a yeast exerting a beneficial influence on the people everywhere.

Once again the special status of the Levites comes to the fore. Because they had been set apart for the special work of the tabernacle, they were not to receive a normal inheritance among the Israelites. Yet they needed a place to live. The Lord therefore arranged that forty-eight cities scattered throughout the whole land should be assigned to the Levites. The cities were to have land around them for tilling (up to 1500 feet from the city wall) and for grazing (up to 3000 feet from the city wall).

This was the Lord's way of providing for the Levites. At the same time he provided that the people who worked at the tabernacle would also be scattered throughout the land. They could then act as models and teachers for all the people of the land.

PREPARATIONS AT THE JORDAN

Life as Individuals

As in other parts of this book, the Lord does not deal only with the issues that affected the whole nation. His concern always reaches down to the level of the individual. Even in preparing for the time when the land would be conquered and occupied the Lord showed his concern for individuals. One aspect was providing cities of refuge for the individuals who had accidentally killed someone. Such people could be kept safe from the family avenger by fleeing to a city of refuge. Another evidence of God's concern for individuals again involved the daughters of Zelophehad. Previously the Lord had decreed that they should receive the inheritance their father would have had. At this point other members of the tribe asked the question whether the tribe would lose the land if the daughters of Zelophehad would marry outside of their tribe. The Lord indicated that they were to marry within the tribe or forfeit their right to the land.

Cities of Refuge

6"Six of the towns you give the Levites will be cities of refuge, to which a person who has killed someone may flee. In addition, give them forty-two other towns. 7In all you must give the Levites forty-eight towns, together with their pasturelands. 8The towns you give the Levites from the land the Israelites possess are to be given in proportion to the inheritance of each tribe: Take many towns from a tribe that has many, but few from one that has few."

9Then the LORD said to Moses: 10"Speak to the Israelites and say to them: 'When you cross the Jordan into Canaan, 11select some towns to be your cities of refuge, to which a person who has killed someone accidentally may flee. [12]They will be places of refuge from the avenger, so that a person accused of murder may not die before he stands trial before the assembly. [13]These six towns you give will be your cities of refuge. [14]Give three on this side of the Jordan and three in Canaan as cities of refuge. [15]These six towns will be a place of refuge for Israelites, aliens and any other people living among them, so that anyone who has killed another accidentally can flee there.

[16] 'If a man strikes someone with an iron object so that he dies, he is a murderer; the murderer shall be put to death. [17]Or if anyone has a stone in his hand that could kill, and he strikes someone so that he dies, he is a murderer; the murderer shall be put to death. [18]Of if anyone has a wooden object in his hand that could kill, and he hits someone so that he dies, he is a murderer; the murderer shall be put to death. [19]The avenger of blood shall put the murderer to death; when he meets him, he shall put him to death. [20]If anyone with malice aforethought shoves another or throws something at him intentionally so that he dies [21]or if in hostility he hits him with his fist so that he dies, that person shall be put to death; he is a murderer. The avenger of blood shall put the murderer to death when he meets him.

[22] 'But if without hostility someone suddenly shoves another or throws something at him unintentionally [23]or, without seeing him, drops a stone on him that could kill him, and he dies, then since he was not his enemy and he did not intend to harm him, [24]the assembly must judge between him and the avenger of blood according to these regulations. [25]The assembly must protect the one accused of murder from the avenger of blood and send him back to the city of refuge to which he fled. He must stay there until the death of the high priest, who was anointed with the holy oil.

[26] 'But if the accused ever goes outside the limits of the city of refuge to which he has fled [27]and the avenger of blood finds him outside the city, the avenger of blood may kill the accused without being guilty of murder. [28]The accused must stay in his city of refuge until the death of the high priest; only after the death of the high priest may he return to his own property.

²⁹" 'These are to be legal requirements for you throughout the generations to come, wherever you live.

³⁰" 'Anyone who kills a person is to be put to death as a murderer only on the testimony of witnesses. But no one is to be put to death on the testimony of only one witness.

³¹" 'Do not accept a ransom for the life of a murderer, who deserves to die. He must surely be put to death.

³²" 'Do not accept a ransom for anyone who has fled to a city of refuge and so allow him to go back and live on his own land before the death of the high priest.

³³" 'Do not pollute the land where you are. Bloodshed pollutes the land, and atonement cannot be made for the land on which blood has been shed, except by the blood of the one who shed it. ³⁴Do not defile the land where you live and where I dwell, for I, the LORD, dwell among the Israelites.' "

Six cities from the forty-eight that belonged to the Levites were to be designated as cities of refuge. Three of these cities were to be east of the Jordan and three west of the Jordan.

The special benefit of the city of refuge was that it was to be a safe place for a person who insisted that he had accidentally killed someone. On the basis of the claim of accidental manslaughter the person could enter the city of refuge. He would be safe there until he had a chance to stand trial before the assembly.

Closely associated with the idea of cities of refuge is the concept about "the avenger." The avenger of blood was a person designated from among the relatives of the dead person. He was appointed to carry out the death penalty on the person who had killed the relative. It was from fear of the avenger of blood that the person responsible for the death of another would flee to the city of refuge. To be protected by the city of refuge the person charged with murder had to stay within the confines of the city. If he left the city of refuge, however, the avenger of blood could execute him with impunity.

On the other hand, when the high priest died, any person who had been allowed to continue in a city of refuge under the judgment of accidental manslaughter could again go free. In a way this shows how the high priest prefigures the work of Christ, our great High Priest, whose death releases us from all sin and punishment.

The balance of the chapter deals with the definitions of premeditated and accidental murder. Having something in hand that was capable of killing, when there had been some previous malice, was evidence that it was a premeditated murder. Malice aforethought was defined as shoving, throwing or hitting with the fist when hostility had been previously shown. But when there was no previous anger and the tool or stone was intended for some other purpose, accidental murder was presumed.

If it was determined that there was intent to kill, the murderer was to be put to death. There was to be no exception to this punishment for reason of personality or money. Even fleeing to a city of refuge did not save a person from the punishment for premeditated murder. In this judgment there was, however, the safeguard that no person could be executed on the basis of circumstantial evidence. There had to be two witnesses. To this rule there also were to be no exceptions. There could also be no exception to the requirement for execution once a person had been properly condemned for murder.

When a murder occurred even the land where the murder took place was considered defiled. Only by punishing the murderer could the defilement of the land be removed. But more important than the punishment was the motivation to avoid the sin. The Lord here reminded the people that he was also living in the land and therefore the people should avoid offending him.

Since God was present in that land, can you imagine the horror God must have felt when in that very land his one and only Son was arraigned and killed through judicial murder? It is an act of remarkable grace that God did not cause more than darkness to come over the earth during the time his Son was on the cross.

Inheritance of Zelophehad's Daughters

36 The family heads of the clan of Gilead son of Makir, the son of Manasseh, who were from the clans of the descendants of Joseph, came and spoke before Moses and the leaders, the heads of the Israelite families. ²They said, "When the LORD commanded my lord to give the land as an inheritance to the Israelites by lot, he ordered you to give the inheritance of our brother Zelophehad to his daughters. ³Now suppose they marry men from other Israelite tribes; then their inheritance will be taken from our ancestral inheritance and added to that of the tribe they marry into. And so part of the inheritance allotted to us will be taken away. ⁴When the Year of Jubilee for the Israelites comes, their inheritance will be added to that of the tribe into which they marry, and their property will be taken from the tribal inheritance of our forefathers."

⁵Then at the LORD's command Moses gave this order to the Israelites: "What the tribe of the descendants of Joseph is saying is right. ⁶This is what the LORD commands for Zelophehad's daughters: They may marry anyone they please as long as they marry within the tribal clan of their father. ⁷No inheritance in Israel is to pass from tribe to tribe, for every Israelite shall keep the tribal land inherited from his forefathers. ⁸Every daughter who inherits land in any Israelite tribe must marry someone in her father's tribal clan, so that every Israelite will possess the inheritance of his fathers. ⁹No inheritance may pass from tribe to tribe, for each Israelite tribe is to keep the land it inherits."

¹⁰So Zelophehad's daughters did as the LORD commanded Moses. ¹¹Zelophehad's daughters — Mahlah, Tirzah, Hoglah,

Milcah and Noah — married their cousins on their father's side. [12]They married within the clans of the descendants of Manasseh son of Joseph, and their inheritance remained in their father's clan and tribe.

The five daughters of Zelophehad were again at center stage. Under the inheritance laws of the Israelites land would normally belong to the man in the family. If, however, there were no sons in a family and a daughter had inherited some land from her father, it would become the land of the husband when she married.

An earlier regulation had provided that the five daughters of the deceased Zelophehad were to inherit the land that Zelophehad would have inherited (Numbers 27:1-11). This caused some concern for other members of the tribe. They presented the issue to Moses and the leaders. If the daughters of Zelophehad married outside of the tribe of Manasseh the land would then be transferred to the land of the tribe to which the husbands belonged. The net result would be that the territory of the tribe of Manasseh would be diminished.

For this situation and for all similar situations the Lord decided that the woman who inherits land would be required to marry within the tribe into which she was born. She could marry anyone, so long as it was within the tribe.

The Lord chose to give precedence to keeping the identity of the tribes as well as keeping the lands within the tribe. This still meant that there were several thousand men that the daughters of Zelophehad could choose from. Certainly their ownership of land did not detract from their desirability as wives.

Once again the Lord showed that he does not consider only the cosmic problems. He knows and cares about the problems of each individual person. In God's eyes no one is unimportant. He will do for them what is exactly right for them.

Conclusion

13These are the commands and regulations the LORD gave through Moses to the Israelites on the plains of Moab by the Jordan across from Jericho.

The book closes with a summary statement that refers to the directives that the Lord gave at the Jordan River. How clearly the Lord knew the needs of his people! How marvelously he had provided for them over the years! How wisely he looked ahead to the situation in Canaan and provided for those circumstances! Truly all was in readiness for Israel's entry into the Promised Land, the land flowing with milk and honey. All that remained were the farewell discourses of Moses and the death of this great spiritual leader. That is the subject matter of the next book, Deuteronomy.

"The LORD is with us," Caleb had asserted in faith years earlier. Even during the wandering in the wilderness the Lord protected the nation and kept it intact. Hostile nations, poisonous snakes, a conniving prophet, temptations to idolatry and adultery could not deflect God from his purpose. He was ready to bring his chosen nation into the Promised Land.

The Lord had brought the very children, whom the unbelieving generation assumed would be killed, to the banks of the Jordan. As they looked across the river to the Promised Land, they had every reason to join with believers in all ages and exclaim: "The LORD is with us!"

EXODUS

Mediterranean Sea

Byblos

Sidon

Laish

Hazor

Merom

Bashan

Jordan

Edrei

Amorites

Shechem

Jabbok

Shiloh

Gibeon Ai

Jericho

Heshbon

Jebus

Hebron

Mt. Nebo

Lachish

Dead Sea

Gaza

Arnon

CANAAN

MOAB

Hormah

Arad

Zered

"Reed" Sea?

Pi Hahiroth (port)

Baal Zephon?

Migdol (fort)

Mt. Hor?

Zin

Kadesh

Punon

EDOM

Rameses

Shur

Amalekites

Paran

EGYPT

Goshen

Etham?

Succoth

Pithom

On

Marah

Ezion Geber

Memphis

Elim

Midian

Sin

Dophkah

Kibroth Hattaavah

Rephidim

Hazeroth

Mt. Sinai

Taberah?

Sinai

Red Sea

Many locations along the Exodus route are tentative. This is true of places in the Nile Delta, of the exact location of the passage through the sea, and of places in the Sinai peninsula. The route shown reflects a faithful reading of the biblical text and the latest archaeological knowledge.

75

miles